EU Procurement: Legal Precedents and their Impact

A look at some of the quirkier and more interesting legal cases around EU procurement and how they have affected tendering practice

by
Andrew Shorter

First edition published by Cambridge Academic, The Studio, High Green, Gt. Shelford, Cambridge CB22 5EG.

ISBN 1-903-499-78-8
978-1-903499-78-8

Printed and bound in the United Kingdom by
4edge Ltd, 7a Eldon Way Industrial Estate, Hockley, Essex, SS5 4AD.

Contents – List of Topics

Dedication

This, my second book, is also dedicated to my family because they enjoyed the first one so much ...

About the author

Author of '*The Definitive Beginners Guide to Tendering and EU Procurement*', Andrew Shorter has worked in construction and procurement for over 30 years. Working with Local Authorities, ALMOs and Housing Associations, his experience in this sector includes all aspects of EU and non-EU procurement and contract management. Andrew has worked as a procurement adviser, practitioner and trainer and continues to do so.

EU Procurement: Legal Precedents and their Impact

Preface

This book explains the impact that some key legal decisions may have on your daily procurement practices: whilst it aims at being readable and at times amusing, it hopes to set some of the requirements of the Procurement Regulations into a practical context and help those tendering to navigate their way through what to some must at first seem like a legal minefield. It isn't, but it does demand thought and care.

In addition, it will look at some of the more recent pieces of legislation, purely to help you keep abreast of any changes to your current practice that these new legal requirements may demand. Not only will the precedents and requirements explained herein guide you towards safer and more compliant procurement, it will also, hopefully, enable you to better understand the implications when someone names a case on which current good practice is based. It may even, dare I say, enable you to better participate in discussions on EU legislation at dinner parties and with your peers.

Key to the value of this book is being able to find what you want. The assumption is that this book will not be read from cover to cover as it would were it some tense thriller: interesting as some of the cases might be, I'll concede that none of them are that. So, to assist with your search, there is a standard index and a list of cases at the back of the book, and an alphabetical contents table at the front that will enable you to search for chapters by specific topics, with cross references to other topics where they apply.

To follow this principle, I have not tried to cover the topics in any order of perceived importance: all legal interpretations are important if and when they apply to your circumstances. Instead, the order of play for precedents follows the alphabetical list of topics and the chapters on specific pieces of legislation are at the end – again in the same order as they are listed in the page of contents.

Further to this, I suggest you browse the opening lines of each chapter in order to understand exactly what is meant by the 'topics' listed in the contents page – the topics are my own interpretations of the key areas of impact of each case.

You will see that I occasionally quote verbatim the judges' comments: this is where I feel the statement is of particular interest. You will also find I make my own comments on cases at times and I present some 'lessons learned' at the end of each chapter. However, I must point out that these *are* purely personal comments and observations on my part and should not be taken as any form of legal advice or guidance. Probably, from what I say, this will be obvious.

Each chapter will guide you to the official reports of the cases cited. These reports do not always make good reading, but it may be that you want a more precise understanding of a case and its outcome than that which I have afforded in this book.

Lastly, this book assumes you have at least a fundamental knowledge of procurement in general and EU procurement in particular. If you don't, you know where to look...[1]

1.See Footnote 2.

Introduction

Legislation – Acts, Regulations, Directives, etc. - lays down the law but it is the cases that get decided in court that establish *how* the law actually works in practice – that is, how it is interpreted and so how it should be applied. It is this interpretation of procurement law that determines how we, as procurement practitioners, have to go about our daily work to ensure we do not transgress. The core purpose of this book is to look at some of these interpretations and see how we heed them.

In my previous book[2] I made it clear that it was not a book on law – and it wasn't – but it could not avoid paying a great deal of attention to the legislation surrounding tendering in the public sector and making many references to it. It therefore occurred to me that perhaps a book covering more of the basics of the law surrounding EU procurement, explaining what it means in laymen's terms, might be a useful supplement to that original volume.

This again is a book for procurement practitioners, not lawyers, because it is not a book that deeply analyses legal cases. Instead, it explains, by topic, how certain aspects of EU procurement need to be practiced in the light of recent judgements or parts of a judgement. It will therefore be found that some cases are not necessarily covered wholly or in any great detail, but references are provided to facilitate this level of further research if wanted.

Court cases primarily interpret the law with respect to a particular set of circumstances and the courts' interpretation in any particular case will generally establish the way forward for future procurements in similar circumstances: in other words, it sets a *precedent* and it is the key precedents that we will be looking at in this book – the ones that are most frequently encountered and those that have had the greatest impact on the daily practice of EU procurement.

---

2. *The Definitive Beginner's Guide to Tendering and EU Procurement* published June 2012, Cambridge Academic

Sometimes, just reading the Regulations isn't quite enough and this book is here to help.

As well as looking at legal interpretations, I have included brief commentaries on some specific pieces of legislation. My criteria for inclusion in this eclectic collection have been that they are recent – and so probably fairly new to some people – and/or they have an impact that is key to the world of procurement. On these bases, it is vital to have an understanding of what they require, and in plain English.

As a further support, each chapter has a lessons learned paragraph; headed *"What it means"*, these paragraphs cast a high-level eye over the chapters' contents, flag up key points and formulate some tips on procurement practice emanating from them. Again, these paragraphs are not exhaustive but meant as a steer in the right direction; they are intended to serve as a guide on what you might need to consider in light of the cases' outcomes and perhaps take into account in your future procurements.

All this having been said, I will maintain yet again that this is not a law book: it is a practitioner's guide on working within EU tendering law, primarily providing guidance and advice in the light of the more important legal outcomes and precedents to come from the European (and other) Courts.

Cases may appear in more than one chapter: this is because, most often, cases go to court on more than one issue and an interesting case may well serve to illustrate the courts' views on more than one aspect of procurement. Hopefully, the index and contents tables will help you navigate through any such apparent duplication.

This having been said, I do not claim to have covered even nearly all of the precedents of which you may need to be aware in your daily procurement activities. The eclectic choice of decisive moments in procurement case law has been entirely personal and I apologise for the omission of any cases that may have helped you, had they been included. In turn, I hope that the ones I have covered are both useful and interesting and indexed in such a way that they can be found easily and, having been found, their implications explained in a readable and practical manner.

Precedents can be interesting (yes – honestly), and often have quirks: I hope you enjoy reading about them and find this book helps you along the way to safer procurements.

CHAPTER 1 – AGREED TERMS

Let's start with an easy one, beginning with 'A'.

What are Agreed Terms?
Agreed Terms are just what they say – the terms of trade (or contract) agreed between two parties. To us it is probably obvious that agreeing terms is vital to any deal or commission and as procurement people we put a lot of effort into laying down what these terms are.

However, sometimes slips do happen and also, when seeking quotes instead of actually tendering for services, it is often the case that the vendor's terms of trading are adopted and the person seeking the quote may not be aware of this.

Problems can arise...

The problems that such misunderstandings[3] can create were considered in the case of GHSP Inc v AB Electronic Ltd.

GHSP Inc. v AB Electronic Ltd
GHSP Inc. (GHSP) supplied electro-mechanical parts to Ford, and these parts contained components made by a firm called AB Electronics (AB). Unfortunately, Ford suffered quite substantial losses when the parts supplied by GHSP were found to be faulty and this was deemed to be due to a component supplied, in turn, by AB. The question arose – who was responsible for, and so liable for, Ford's losses?

A preliminary hearing, established to determine which party's terms formed the contract, found that GHSP's standard terms and conditions held that AB would have unlimited liability under the contract. Unfortunately, AB's terms & conditions provided that they would have almost no liability: one 'contract' but two perceived sets of terms and conditions!

---

3. See also Chapter 21 on misunderstandings and mistakes in other contexts.

The quirk here (if that is what it is) is that both parties thought they were working to agreed terms (their own terms), yet in fact neither of them were: neither of them had accepted the other's terms and conditions, so in reality neither set of T&Cs specifically applied.

The Court held that the contract had been concluded (i.e. set up or established) when AB agreed to supply the components in accordance with a production schedule made up by GHSP. Following along this line of the basis of trade, the Court ruled that the components had been supplied – in other words the contract had been conducted – on the terms (albeit implied) of the Sale of Goods Act 1979 (SGA) and because of this the supplier (AB) had unlimited liability for claims arising from the products being found defective.

What this means

> The health warning here is the obvious one – make sure you know what T&Cs you are signing up to. Of course, your own are preferred but this is not always possible (with goods purchased under an RFQ[4], for instance)

> When purchasing under another company's T&Cs ensure you (a) know what they are, (b) where they leave you if there is a problem in the future and (c) do not accept the terms if they leave you or your organisation excessively vulnerable. It is likely you can negotiate a variation to standard T&Cs if the seller wants the business, but if the purchase is relatively small, keep any thoughts of such negotiations in proportion

> Of course, in the case above, the purchaser (GHSP) succeeded at law and the vendor (AB) was found to be liable under the SGA: lucky for GHSP but not for AB. In probably all similar instances you would also be the purchaser, but even so you may not be so lucky if you do not know under what terms you are entering into a contract

---

4. RFQ – Request for a Quote

Cases:

- *GHSP Inc v AB Electronic Ltd [2010] EWHC 1828 (Comm) -*
  Case No: 2008

CHAPTER 2 – BONDS

What are Bonds?
For our purposes we will look primarily at Performance Bonds. A Performance Bond is like an insurance policy, specifically drawn up to provide cover in the event that a company can no longer provide the contracted service or otherwise fulfil their contractual obligations. To meet the consequential costs incurred by the client, it is normal to ask for a Bond with a value of 10% of the contract sum. If there are reasons why this figure ought to be higher, it can be so, but it will cost more. Bonds cost money- normally about 10% of the Bond value – and the client will pay for this, either as a directly identified cost or absorbed within the tendered sum.

A Bond is designed purely to cover losses - the costs incurred rectifying the situation when a provider – for example – goes out of business: it will not cover the cost of completing the remaining contract. You can claim the (additional) costs incurred if you use an interim provider (for example, to cover an essential service) and the costs of re-tendering the service, but these costs have to be ascertainable, that is real and provable. Bonds do not cover damages.

Bonds are required or not depending on the value of the contract, the level of risk in it and the nature of the contract itself. It may be that you require a Bond specifically to cover risks you see associated with the company you are appointing (this has been known).

You would certainly ask for a Bond for a high-value contract and for one providing essential services (primarily you would want it to pay for instant cover).

Bonds are either 'On Demand' or 'Conditional'. I imagine that you will rarely come across On-Demand Bonds – they are normally used in very large, international contracts and mainly in the oil and gas industries. They are what they say – the person in whose interest the Bond is secured can demand payment at any time and often with little or no proof of cause or reason, so the risks attached to them are obvious.

In July 2010, The Uniform Rules for Demand Guarantee (known as URDG), published by the International Chamber of Commerce (ICC), came into force. These Rules were designed to be included in an On-Demand Bond (if wanted - they do not have to be) and lay down specific requirements as part of the claim procedure – including setting out in writing the basis on which the claim is made.

Even so, On-Demand Bonds are extremely onerous, far more so than Conditional Bonds, and they should be avoided at all costs. Let us look at an example.

Simon Carves Ltd v. Ensus UK Ltd
A case at the Technology and Construction Court (TCC) in January 2011 looked at an instance where an injunction was sought to stop a claim being made against an On-Demand bond when it was considered unjustified. In Simon Carves Ltd (Carves) v. Ensus UK Ltd (Ensus), Carves was commissioned to construct an ethanol plant and, in keeping with the contract terms, an On-Demand Bond was issued by Carves' bank in Ensus' interest.

The 'trick' to protect Carves was that, within the contract terms, once Ensus' Project Manager had issued an Acceptance Certificate for Carves' work, the Bond would become null and void. However, several months after the Acceptance Certificate had been issued and Carves thought they were safe, Ensus made a call on the Bond.

Carves immediately sought an injunction to halt the call on the Bond pending a determination at court as to whether the call on the Bond was justified. The TCC actually upheld the injunction and delayed payment on the Bond until the demand was justified (or not) through the courts.

This case allowed that, as the underlying contract clearly prevented a claim being made, then such a claim could be held in abeyance by the court pending an outcome of the deciding case. This was an extremely significant decision because, hitherto, an On-Demand Bond could only be stopped in its tracks if a fraudulent claim was alleged.

Even so – avoid On-Demand Bonds. That is the health warning.

Conditional bonds are much more commonly used and are much safer as they can only be called upon in the event of an actual default by the contractor and they normally require documentary evidence of losses to support any claim made against them. Sometimes legal action through the courts is required to secure the due proceeds but, so long as the Bond is from a reputable provider, it will serve to cover the eligible losses.

Some organisations demand that Bonds use their own standard wording so as to ensure the level of 'cover' the client requires and the terms on which they can be realised (for example, a period of validity after completion of the contract) and this can sometimes cause problems with the Bond supplier, who may want alternative wording. Such issues are normally resolved, albeit with the involvement of your legal department (because the Bond is a legal document), but it does mean the tender and award process may be delayed in the meantime.

Why are some organisations so particular? Because, in reality, the words bond and guarantee, for example, are meaningless in law and the wording of the document in question is vital.

So what's in a name? Let us look at a splendid example.

Trafalgar House Construction (Regions) Ltd v General Surety & Guarantee Co. Ltd
In this case a claim against a bond went to court and the judge declared he considered the bond to be a Conditional Bond; the Appeal Court then ruled it was an On-Demand Bond. The case

eventually went to the House of Lords who, as the highest court in the land, had the final say, and they concluded it was a guarantee!

The document in question was simply entitled 'Bond' (not a lot of use) and the case serves to illustrate the importance of the wording. This is particularly so because of the large number of different types of 'guarantee' that can be drawn up: as well as On-Demand and Conditional Bonds you can also have documents entitled simple bonds, performance bonds, conditional-demand bonds, bank guarantees, demand guarantees, default bonds, performance guarantees, surety bonds, surety guarantees, parent company guarantees[5]...

These are too many for us to consider (you'll be relieved to hear) but there are two more aspects to this 'warranty' business – LADs and Guarantees - that I would like to spend some time on in a later chapter.

What this means

> Taking out a Bond or other surety to protect your contract seems simple enough, but there are some things to consider

> First thing – is it a necessary requirement?

> The cost of the bond may need to be taken into account during the evaluation process: whilst the cost might normally be contained within (or covered by) the tendered contract price, bidders can be asked to identify it as a separate sum

> More importantly, making sure you ask for the right kind of surety is essential and the wording has to be right, formulated to meet your needs

---

5. Parent Company Guarantee (PCG) - where a holding company provides a guarantee for a subsidiary who has won a contract. Normally called-for in any instance where a winning bidder has a holding or parent company. If the parent company declines, be alarmed!

> Always make sure any Bond is underwritten by a legitimate source: it is hard claiming on a Bond underwritten by a company in the Cayman Islands who are no longer there when you need them...

> Always ask for a PCG if the bidder has a holding company. The cost of a PCG is zero

> In other words – when demanding a bond (or other surety), make sure it is precisely what you want

---

Cases:

- *Simon Carves Ltd v. Ensus UK Ltd, Court of Appeal, Technology and Construction Court 2011 – EWHC 657 (TCC) - Case No: HT-11-67*
- *Trafalgar House Construction (Regions) Ltd v General Surety & Guarantee Co. Ltd [1995] 3 WLR 204; (1994) 66 BLR 42*

CHAPTER 3 – BREACH OF CONTRACT

What is Breach of Contract?
An easy question, of course. A breach of contract is precisely what it says – when you do not fulfil your obligations under an agreement. If you are unable to do so because your firm has gone broke, then a Bond may be called in to help put matters right- providing one is in place (see Chapter 2). If the matter is 'simply' that you have not done what you were supposed to do, then recourse through the courts may be the only remedy...

This is a common cause of litigation. The case we will look at here is old (1854) but even so is still used to define the 'test' for a case of breach of contract.

Hadley & Another v Baxendale & Others
Hadley was a mill owner who contracted with Baxendale (who was a carrier) to transport a broken mill part to Greenwich for repair. All the while the part was in disrepair the mill failed to function so obviously speed and reliability in the delivery process were of the essence. Unfortunately, Hadley forgot to convey this matter of urgency to Baxendale.

Needless to say (as in all good stories) the part was delivered late and Hadley sued Baxendale for loss of profits. The basis of his claim was that losses were incurred because Baxendale had not delivered (literally) what the contract required.

Cutting to the chase, the Court decided that Baxendale was not liable because the urgency and criticality of the delivery had not been made clear as part of the deal and Baxendale could not have been expected to know this. In essence, and perhaps obviously to us now, Hadley should have made the urgency clear at the time of commission.

The Court, on the back of this, laid down tests for when damages for breach of contract can be recovered, and these tests are still used today. The Court decided that any loss, to be recoverable, must fall into either one of two categories:

a. Direct Losses, namely any that flow directly from the breach of contract (for example, retail stock not delivered cannot be resold and so a loss of profit directly ensues)
b. Indirect or Consequential Losses, namely losses that in all probability stem from the breach and which were known to the parties (and certainly the party who is in breach) when the contract was struck. (In the example of the retail goods above, an indirect loss may be the additional storage cost of goods pending their eventual sale).

Direct and Indirect Losses may at times seem hard to distinguish – they do not distinguish between the *type* of loss incurred but more on how *obvious* or *direct* the loss was to the breach (meaning the 'oh, I never thought of that' type of loss is an indirect loss).

Whilst the 'tests' are largely agreed and still applied – albeit over 160 years later – the subsequent judgement is largely a matter of individual interpretation and indirect losses are not so easily recoverable: they were not foreseeable and so not explicitly part of the contracted liability.

Thus commercial certainty is low in such cases: it is therefore a matter of establishing contract clauses that lay down clearly what damages can and cannot be claimed in the event of a breach. The more specific you are in your contract, the less you will be at the mercy of a Court's interpretation of the two tests; the problem is, 'unforeseeable' losses are hard to foresee...

Remember, though, the more you transfer liability onto the other party, the more tender costs will escalate. An assessment of risk and a degree of reasonableness should prevail.

What this means

> When playing the 'breach of contract' card you need to make

sure that, above all, the contract provides for such a claim insofar as there *are* clauses that have been breached: in other words, has the provider simply not provided a service that you did not ask for in the first place?

> You will need to be able to demonstrate losses if you are to benefit from any such claim and there are established (Baxendale) tests used by the courts for assessing direct and indirect (or consequential) losses. Does your claim pass either of these tests?

> You can 'clause' your way out of any doubt by including stringent contractual requirements but you must balance this temptation by understanding that the more ominous the contract terms, the higher the price will be. I would think a consideration of risk would be a good way forward to achieve the required balance

---

Cases:

• *Hadley & Another v Baxendale & Others, High Court, [1854] EWHC Exch J70 (23 February 1854)*

CHAPTER 4 – CHALLENGES & OUT OF TIME

What is a Challenge and why is timing so important?
Challenges can be levelled at either the PQQ or the tender stage; I shall look specifically at the raising of challenges at the tender stage (which is, of course, the most critical stage), the importance of the timescales attached to them and the Courts' approach to reaching a judgement.

It must be remembered that the legal timescales for bringing a challenge have been changed since some of these cases went to court, so some of the detail, whilst right at the time, may not apply under current legislation. The principles of the judgements prevail, however, and so still serve to illustrate the points being made.

A Challenge in the context of an EU Procurement means that a party to the tender process raises an objection to an outcome on the basis that some infringement has occurred. In plain English this means that a firm that fails to pass a pre-selection process or who does not win a tender may raise an objection on the grounds that something has not been done right.

Challenges have always been a pain in the neck but they were given a particularly sharp edge when the Remedies Directive, introduced in December 2009 (just in time for Christmas!), gave the courts serious added powers should a challenge be upheld.

Chapter 30 covers the Remedies Directive in some detail and a specific case is looked at in Chapter 17 on Ineffectiveness, but I hope I am not spoiling the surprise when I warn you that, in certain circumstances, the Remedies Directive *instructs* courts that the only course of action in the case of a successful challenge is to cancel (yes – cancel) the contract. Of course, I need not tell you that, were a tender of yours to be the subject of such a challenge and the challenge resulted in a cancellation, your career may experience a hiccup of some magnitude. That having been said, even the best of us stand the risk of such a challenge, no matter how careful we are or how clever we think we are.

A prime case in recent history is the one where Richard Branson challenged the outcome of a tender for the West Coast Rail Route. In this instance, the matter did not get to court but was dealt with by the Department for Transport (DfT) and was followed up by the Laidlaw Report[6]. Nevertheless, lawyers were involved (of course) and it serves as a good illustration of a challenge at time of tender and the potential outcomes.

Virgin Challenge to DfT
The tender was for the lucrative InterCity West Coast (ICWC) passenger rail franchise and ITT documents were issued in January 2012. Shortly after their issue, the project team (which included DfT[7] Officials and Lawyers) recognised that the part of the evaluation model to be used to assess the financial resilience of a bidder's proposal (i.e. the franchisee's ability to sustain the required level of service over the required period of time, even in times of a fall in business) was flawed in that it was a model designed for internal use by the assessors and it had not been declared openly to bidders.

Immediately, the obvious issues of transparency arose and it was decided to issue Supplementary Guidance to offset the omission. So, towards the end of February 2012, the DfT issued Supplementary Guidance (a clarification) and a 'ready reckoner' that showed bidders how their contingency provisions to cover financial risk (for example, in the event of a drop-off in revenue) would be considered. The guidance explained:

> *"The DfT has used the DfT GDP Resilience Model and assumptions from its own comparator model to give*

---

6. Laidlaw Report: Inquiry into the lessons learned for the Department for Transport from the InterCity West Coast Competition
7. DfT – Department for Transport

bidders an indication as to the size of SLF[8] that might be required at different margins or levels of risk adjustment. The figures in the table below are for illustrative purposes only and should not be regarded as the confirmed level of financial support that might be required in different levels of bid margin."

In other words, the DfT provided a table (the 'ready reckoner') indicating what level of financial provision might be required but the actual evaluation model – how they would assess the proposed level of provision - was still not declared. In retrospect it seems that, instead of addressing the problem, they were digging a deeper hole.

Unfortunately, things became a little worse when, at the time of evaluation, it was decided not to use the declared method at all and instead to have the SLF submissions assessed on the basis of 'a view' of the CAC (Contract Award Committee) – in other words, the DfT's *view* of the appropriate level of required capital. Still digging.

There were other problems, too: albeit it was explained to bidders that the figures in the ready reckoner were a guide, they were in fact low by about 50%: a variance which could be construed as misleading.

And so it went on.

Of significance to us is the fact that Virgin did not level the challenge under the EU Procurement Regulations and the implication of this is that Virgin considered the process legally 'sound'; instead they went to the High Court to secure a judicial review on the basis that the bidding process was flawed in that relevant matters had not been factored in, resulting in an erroneous outcome. So note: getting the process wrong is illegal, but getting the process right but doing it badly is not. Virgin therefore required a higher authority to review the process and agree that it would reach the wrong conclusion.

8. SLF – Subordinated Loan Facility – is that part of the risk capital bidders would lose - or sacrifice - if they failed to meet the terms of their contract. This sum needs to be a provision within the contract's capital funding.

Virgin therefore challenged that the tender process was flawed, in that the assessment of the SLF was flawed, and that the figures submitted by the declared winner of the bid were erroneous to the point where their bid was, in reality, unsustainable. An investigation showed that this was, in fact, the case.

At this stage, and under the circumstances, there was no alternative but to abandon the whole tender process with a view to starting again. There was little doubt that all the bidders would seek redress for the vast expenditure they had each undertaken to prepare their bids. Lucky old taxpayers!

There were those who initially thought Virgin was being a poor loser in the face of not winning something they really wanted – the ICWC – but once the facts emerged there were few procurement professionals around who were not quite amazed at the way the tender and the subsequent evaluation had been carried out. There lies a lesson.

Avoiding too much of the minutiae of the case (for there is more), the whole issue serves to illustrate some key pointers regarding challenges:

a) You must explain, at time of tender, how you are going to carry out your evaluation process in a clear and transparent manner.
b) You must then carry out the evaluation in the manner you have declared.
c) If you have contravened the basic requirements of transparency and openness, any challenge will be virtually indefensible.
d) It may well be that, on consideration, you find a challenge is correct. In such circumstances you may be best advised to accept the challenge and not take it 'to the wire' and try and win a defence. The DfT realised they were wrong and conceded: they suffered criticism and embarrassment but did avoid enormous legal costs on top of the costs already incurred.
e) No matter how high-powered or how numerous your resources are, you should not be complacent: the same rules apply

whether you are tendering a contract for six new printers or a whole railway service. Get it wrong and there could be trouble – big trouble.

It is a fact[9] that over 80% of challenges are based on process: get the process right and in most cases you will be challenge free. Most cases.

What hope, then, if you are challenged? Remember, being asked for feedback and having the tender outcome questioned is not a challenge. In the majority (if not all) cases, if your process is sound and consistent and evaluation criteria have been correctly applied (both aspects of which are within your control), once feedback has been provided, bidders will generally accept the outcome, even if grudgingly. Taking the matter further would blot their copybook with you as a potential future client and will cost them time and money.

The corollary of this is, if they *do* progress a challenge, you can reckon they are pretty sure of their ground and you need to be prepared. On this basis, read bullet point (d) above again.

Sometimes, challenges can be headed off at the pass and you need to be wary of 'taking on' a challenge when it ought not, in law, to have been raised. A case in point is Mermec UK Ltd v. Network Rail Infrastructure Ltd when the legislation acted (for once) in favour of the client, not the bidder.

Mermec UK Ltd v. Network Rail Infrastructure Ltd
Interestingly enough, this is another railway one. I think this is just a coincidence but there are other similarities, too. The case follows in the path of the more well-known Sita and Uniplex cases, which we shall look at later.

Mermec UK Ltd (Mermec) were bidding to provide a specific type of rail inspection regime (the details are not relevant here

---

9. *My* fact – but a sound estimate nevertheless.

unless you're a railway enthusiast – and I'm not) to Network Rail Infrastructure Ltd (NRI). Mermec were not successful and duly received the Alcatel[10] letter advising them of where their bid was deficient. The standstill period was due to end at midnight on 3rd October 2011.

Mermec's solicitors wrote to NRI on the 1st October asking for more details of the way in which the bid had been scored. They reserved the right to start proceedings under Regulation 47F (which covers the requirements for instituting proceedings).

Cutting to the chase, communications were exchanged (including a meeting) between Mermec and NRI, all concerning the issue of criteria, sub-criteria and sub-sub-criteria (and – yes – even sub-sub-sub criteria!). The upshot was that on 22nd December 2010 Mermec issued a High Court claim seeking damages for breaches of the Regulations. The Notice was eventually served on 30th December 2010 (everything stops for Christmas).

The grounds for the claim were, in brief:

- Failure to advise Mermec properly of the reasons for the failure of their bid
- Failure of NRI to properly assess Mermec's bid in accordance with the methodology laid down in the ITT (remember Virgin? Although the challenge here is on the basis of process, hence the challenge under EU procurement law)
- Failure by NRI to properly score the winning tender when compared with the evaluation of Mermec's own bid (this without supporting detail as NRI had apparently failed to provide the required information at time of Alcatel. If true, this was naughty).

Network, in defence, requested summary judgment on the basis that the claim was out of time and that most of the claims (not particularly relevant here) were bound to fail anyway. The court

10. Alcatel Letter – see Chapter 4 on Standstill Periods

conceded that, no matter how good and sound the Mermec case was, it was out of time and could not be considered.

The court cited the following reasons:

- Regardless of whether the letter of the 23rd contained enough information, the facts were apparent on that date (remember – the day it was known or ought to have been known...) and so the right to bring a claim began on that day.
- The fact that legal advice was not sought until 1st October is not relevant: the fact that Mermec had knowledge of the relevant facts is sufficient to start the clock ticking.
- The clock started ticking before the 30th September, so the case was clearly lodged out of time.

The court also commented that the matter was entirely within the hands of Mermec and there were no external or other mitigating factors that would or could justify any extension of the timescale (the court has some discretion to extend under special circumstances, which actually are rarely accepted as sufficient cause to extend).

The interesting point about the outcome of the case is that the judgement stated that, however good and arguable the grounds for the claim may have been (*may* have been – see the judge's comments, below), the case could not even be considered because the claim was out of time, albeit by just a few days.

The Regulations clearly state that the time limit for bringing a claim is three months, and the date of service is just that – the date on which the claim is physically served. The court made it clear: "... *there is no point in having a three-month period if what it means is three months plus a further relatively random short period...*"

The ruling also made another interesting point. Mermec argued that they could not enter a claim sooner as they did not, through no fault of their own, have all the required details to hand. The Court's view was that Mermec should have entered the claim initially on the grounds that it felt the process was wrong, albeit not necessarily before or after the Alcatel period had ended. This is a quirk of the Regulations of which you need to be aware.

The Regulations require 10 days' standstill (minimum) for feedback on a bidder's submission. As the Contracting Authority, do not assume that, if you come through those 10 days unscathed you are clear. The Regulations allowed bidders three months to enter a claim *promptly after they become aware of the transgression*[11]. They did not specify that this had to be within the 10-day Standstill period but the requirements needed careful consideration, as you will see as we go on.

Of course, bidders may become aware of the transgression during the 10-day period but with Mermec it took a little longer. Regardless, the 30th December was outside the 3-month period and the court felt they should have lodged their challenge earlier for it to be valid. Count the days then see *Uniplex* that follows.

Mermec may have been upset at losing by what was, after all, a very close margin – their score was 71.7% whereas the successful bidder – Omnicom – scored 72.06%. Whatever reason, it certainly does seem that their claim was, at the least, very ambitious.

The judge[12], apparently, thought the same, saying: *"It would be wholly wrong for this Court to refuse Network Rail's application in relation to such an unpleaded complaint. It has all the hallmark of a perfectly understandable reaction by an employee who was disappointed that his company did not succeed and involves no more than an uncorroborated belief that Mermec could only have been stopped from succeeding by some sort of skullduggery. In football supporter terms, it is no more than a cry of 'we was robbed'."*

---

11. Timescales for a challenge under the EU Regulations is now just 30 days from when the claimant knew or ought to have known of the infringement (an Amendment to the EU Regs dated 2011); an action to set aside an award decision under the Remedies Directive also has to be effected within just 30 days; timescales for instigating a Judicial Review remains at three months. Simple, isn't it?"
12. Mr Justice Akenhead

Moral: if you do get a legal challenge, have a quick look at the calendar – you may just be lucky...

Now let's look at *Uniplex*, then we'll go onto *Varney* and *Sita*. Don't get too excited.

Uniplex UK Ltd v NHS Business Services Authority
This case is a bit like Mermec (it is in the same chapter, after all) but comes at it from a slightly different angle, stating that the time limit for an action to be brought may not start (i.e. need not start) until the time when the Applicant (or bidder) knew, *or ought to have known*, of the alleged breach.

In this instance, Uniplex UK Ltd (Uniplex), received an Alcatel letter on the 22nd November 2007 Advising that the Business Services Authority (NHS) had decided to go with three Framework providers, not with Uniplex who had scored the lowest of all tenderers. The letter also gave details of scores and weightings, etc. Uniplex sought an additional de-brief and NHS provided additional information on 13th December. On 28th January 2008, Uniplex wrote to NHS alleging a number of breaches in the process and stating that the time period in which they had to bring a claim did not start until 13th December 2007.

NHS replied, making it clear the time period ran from 22nd November (the date of the Alcatel letter) but Uniplex still only issued proceedings on 12th March 2008 ("you do the maths", as they say).

The Court of Justice held that the period for bringing proceedings should run from the date on which the claimant knew – or should have known – about the infringement.

Of note here is:

1. The affirmation that action needs to be brought within three months of the date on which the infringement was known or should have been known – *not* the start or end of the Standstill period.

2. In each case we've looked at in this chapter, the claim was for alleged aberration of declared evaluation processes. Check out the chapter on Criteria.

However, the issue of "...or ought to have known..." gives rise to some interesting decisions – take *Varney*, for example.

J Varney & Sons Waste Management Ltd (Varney) v Hertfordshire County Council (Herts)

Varney was somewhat notable in that there had been a run of pro-tenderer (i.e. pro-bidder) judgements but in this case, the judgement went in favour of the Contracting Authority. It also showed a degree of flexibility – or logic – in the decision rather than a dotted-i and crossed-t approach to the interpretation of the Regulations – a move welcomed by Contracting Authorities everywhere.

Varney was a bidder for a waste recycling contract in Hertfordshire, but failed to win. Varney brought two claims regarding the initial procurement and changes to the contracts once they had been awarded (a real danger area – beware: see Chapter 5).

The detailed list of grounds for the claim centred around:

- a failure to disclose criteria and weightings,
- mis-applied criteria relating to a bidder's financial strength,
- accepted bid prices that were abnormally low (and therefore claimed to be unsustainable),
- evaluation inconsistencies and lastly
- failure to enforce contractual requirements once the award had been made.

In a nutshell, Varney was not happy. They were probably even less happy at the court's decision.

The Court found that the claim was out of time: Varney had relied upon the Uniplex case and counted three months from the time they were notified of their failure to win a contract. The Court ruled that Varney would have been aware of – or *ought* to have been aware of

– the lack of detail of the evaluation criteria at the time of ITT and so the time for a claim should have been counted from then.

A key lesson for Contracting Authorities in this is to look at the timescales – is a challenge to your process out of time? The corollary of this is that, had Varney challenged in time they may well have won their case and to counteract this you need to be absolutely transparent in the documents you issue. Make everything absolutely clear in all respects.

The issue of the claim regarding low tenders is an interesting aside to this case and is an issue covered elsewhere in this book. Low bids can be a problem and suicide bidding does go on, so we will give this some consideration later on (see Chapter 25).

Sita UK Limited v Greater Manchester Waste Disposal Authority
In February 2005 the Greater Manchester Waste Disposal Authority (GMWDA) began a tender process for a PFI contract to provide waste disposal facilities and Sita UK Limited (Sita) was one of the final two firms selected to provide a best and final offer. On 26th January 2007 the Greater Manchester Waste Disposal Authority (GMWDA) announced that Viridor Laing was the preferred bidder, leaving Sita as the reserve.

GMWDA negotiated further with Viridor, which led to some changes being made to their offer and a re-evaluation of their bid (a press statement issued in April 2009, announcing the eventual contract with Viridor, made it clear that the contract did vary somewhat from that originally envisaged at time of tender).

GMWDA sent an Alcatel letter to Sita on the 18th April 2008; Sita complained to GMWDA on 21st April concerning their conduct of the tender process and that certain aspects regarding the cost and material aspects of the provision had been changed and that alterations to the documentation relating to the bid had been made. A further letter was sent by GMWDA on the 9th May 2008 re-iterating what had been previously sent.

There was correspondence between GMWDA and Sita, during which Sita offered to submit a revised proposal, but GMWDA persisted with Viridor and entered into contract with them on the 8th April 2009.

On 27th August 2009, Sita started High Court proceedings seeking damages.

As in all these cases, the dates are significant and once again distracted the case from the core arguments of the action. Instead of an argument around poor process, the case hinged around exactly when Sita knew of the alleged infringements and so when the clock actually started ticking on the time in which they had to lodge a claim via the courts.

GMWDA claimed the action should be struck out because the 'clock' should have started ticking on 8th April 2009 when the contract with Viridor was concluded – claiming that Sita should have known about the alleged infringements by then at the latest.

The Court found in favour of GMWDA in that Sita indeed should have known sufficient to bring an action by that date. Sita sought an extension of the time being counted on the grounds that it delayed action whilst seeking further information to support its claim and did not have sufficient knowledge to pursue this claim until 3rd July 2009. However, the Court maintained that, although further alleged breaches were uncovered in July 2009, this knowledge merely supported Sita's original allegations and they knew enough by the 8th of April to commence proceedings.

Interestingly, the Court stated that had Sita, in July, found *different* bases for a claim, then the clock could have started from that time for those particular allegations.

All this in the face of the Court stating clearly that there did, in fact, appear to have been breaches to the proceedings committed by GMWDA.

Thus the case was lost by Sita in the first hearing and it was also dismissed at Appeal.

Moral: watch the clock, whichever side you are on!
And now for something completely different...

R (Buglife) v Natural England
This case hinges around a proposed development project on a site where the work may have had a high environmental impact. National Grid Property Holdings Ltd (National Grid) wanted to build a Business Park on a piece of land on the Isle of Grain owned by Medway Borough Council (Medway). The project would have taken 10 years and provided much-needed employment in the area, but the site, in particular, was one which provided habitats for a range of rare and protected invertebrates including the Brown-banded Carder Bee.

National Grid produced an Environmental Impact Statement (EIS) as part of its outline planning application but this was not very thorough and, as the project would be in four distinct phases, it was agreed that more thorough EISs would be undertaken for each stage.

Natural England was a consultant to the project and eventually a way forward was agreed such that Medway granted outline planning permission for the development.

The Invertebrate Conservation Trust (Buglife) sought a Judicial Review on the granting of this outline permission on the grounds that:

a) The EIS by National Grid was inadequate and insufficiently detailed so that...
b) Medway was not informed enough to make a properly-considered decision, meaning that...
c) Permission was granted without proper measures being in place to mitigate the adverse impact of the development.

The challenge was made by Buglife just two days short of a three-month window counting from the day the outline permission was granted. The questions arose:

1. Had Buglife applied for the Review early enough and, following Uniplex,
2. Was there, in law, a requirement to apply promptly?

Buglife maintained that the Uniplex case decided there was no need for promptness and so the (usual) three months was adequate. Medway countered that Uniplex applied to Procurement Law, and this was a matter of Environmental Law and the EIA Directives specifically.

It is relevant that there were discussions regarding how Medway intended to proceed with National Grid during the course of agreeing detailed planning permission for each stage, and they maintained that adequate provisions, through Environmental Impact Assessments (EIAs), would be agreed as the development progressed.

In the end, the Court refused to quash the outline planning permission but agreed with Buglife that the development needed a succession of EIAs and EISs at the crucial stages, meaning that Buglife in effect was successful in meeting its aims.

On the matter of law, the court decided that the Uniplex decision applied across the board and was not limited to EU Procurement Law and observed that English Law is particularly lax on this point in that this has not been taken into account.

It is also interesting to note that, after the outline permission had been granted, Buglife had assisted the National Grid's consultants in drawing up an ecological survey methodology which went on to help the National Grid in their environmental endeavours, and the court had recognised that this had drained Buglife's resources when bringing their legal action.

What this means

Many of the lessons to be learned from this chapter have been highlighted as we have gone along, but I thought a summary would be useful nevertheless:

> Challenges to a procurement are strictly time-bound. Although the courts *do* have discretion to allow additional time in extenuating circumstances, rarely are the circumstances considered extenuating enough to justify allowing any extra time at all

> Even if the court considers a challenge to be 'correct', if it is out of time it will not be upheld

> If you are challenged (I mean seriously challenged, not simply being asked for feedback or clarification) check the time line first: the clock starts ticking from the time the litigant knew *or should have known* of the claimed infringement – the italicised phrase is of extreme importance – and the time needs to be calculated to the very day

> Timescales vary according to the nature of the challenge (e.g. is it a claim for setting aside the award decision under the Remedies Directive?) so check you are measuring the time against the right legal requirement and also remember that it is counted as calendar days (for example, Christmas is irrelevant)

> Two further points: [i] the 10-day standstill period is irrelevant to the timescales and [ii] legal advice is highly recommended if the challenge persists

---

Cases:

• *Virgin challenge to DfT – Laidlaw Report, 6th December 2012*

- Mermec UK Ltd v Network Rail Infrastructure Ltd [2011] EWHC 1847 (TCC)) 19th July 2011
- *Uniplex UK Ltd v NHS Business Services Authority [2010] EUECJ C-406/08, 28th January 2010*
- *J Varney & Sons Waste Management Ltd v Hertfordshire County Council [2011] EWCA Civ 708, 21st June*
- *Sita UK Limited v Greater Manchester Waste Disposal Authority [2011] 2 CMLR 32, 134 Con LR 1, 24th February*
- *R (Buglife) v Natural England [2011] EWHC 746 (Admin) (30 March 2011) (www.practicallaw.com/0-506-2064) .*

CHAPTER 5 – CHANGES TO CONTRACTS

Why this topic is important
I have emphasised elsewhere the importance of making sure the OJEU Notice reflects the contract that lies ahead: OJEU contents are sacrosanct. The trouble is, over the life of a contract, especially as relationships build up, there can be contract 'creep' because providers tend to be asked to do more and more and the nature of a contract slowly changes until, all of a sudden, it is realised that the contract is not as it started out or – worse - as it was intended.

In EU Procurement Law, this is wrong and it is very clear that a contract variation – or a series of contract variations – can reach the point where the provision becomes a completely different type of contract which should have been tendered in its own right in the first place.

Where this 'tipping point' is can often be open to debate but if market providers feel a variation has led to a contract that they feel they should have had the chance to tender for, they may well raise a challenge. If they do not, the matter may still end up in the ECJ anyway on the basis of breach of the Regulations.

Pressetext Nachrichtenagentur GmbH v Republik Österreich (Bund)
The name is a mouthful, but this is a well-known case, recognised by all as Pressetext. Whilst the circumstances of this case are fairly specific, the judgements and legal advice coming from it are quite far-reaching and form a good guide on the matter of new contract or not.

APA Austria Presse Agentur (APA) had an agreement with the Austrian Government for the provision of various press- and information-related services. This was in 1994 (a while ago but the case is still very relevant today). In 2000, APA established APA-

OTS, a wholly-owned subsidiary that was completely integrated, organisationally and financially.

Some changes in the Agreement with the Austrian Government ensued:

- The terms were altered to reflect Austria's adoption of the Euro in January 2002
- Some charges were rounded down (by a small amount) to accommodate the currency change
- Price indexation was primarily based on the CPI of 1996 but some derogation from this meant that in real terms some prices fell
- A second Agreement effective from 1 January 2006, extended the waiver of the right to terminate the agreement from 31 December 1999 to December 2008
- A discount of 15% on some services was raised to 25%

Pressetext Nachrichtenagentur GmbH (Pressetext) brought a court action on the basis that the new set-up constituted a new contract that should have been tendered on the open market. In response, the Austrian court asked for a steer from the ECJ.

The quirk is that, whilst the agreement dated from before Austria's accession to the EU, once Austria became part of the EU, "the rules" kicked in.

The directives do not define when a contract effectively becomes a new contract but do state that a contract effectively becomes a new contract when it becomes materially different in character from that originally tendered. Material amendments comprise conditions or changes which:

- If they had been part of the original award procedure would have allowed for the admission of bidders other than those who were originally accepted for tender or would have allowed for the acceptance of another bid

- Extend the scope of the contract to encompass services not originally covered
- Put the contractor in a better financial position than the original contract did.

With respect to the Pressetext case, the court found:

- The nature of the new APA-OTS set-up, where APA remained jointly and severally liable and where profits and funds are moved freely between the two parts, indicates that there has been no material change in the supplier – it is ostensibly the service being provided by a subsidiary and so presents no problem. However, had the change been such that the responsibility for the service would have moved to a third party, the situation would have been different and so the contract would have materially changed. This is an interesting point to note when a provider goes into liquidation, for example, and the contract is novated to a third party to continue providing the service: this is a common practice and could be illegal and open to challenge (although the new 2014 Directives clarify this and give more scope for using this useful legal device).
- The currency changes were unavoidable; the adjustments made were minimal and, in fact, to the contractor's detriment, so no contravention took place.
- The original contract had expressly permitted a change of index at a later stage in the contract, so no material change took place.
- There is nothing in the Regulations regarding maximum length of contracts; similarly there is nothing in law preventing a clause agreeing not to terminate a contract for a given period. The court took a view that there had been no move to terminate the contract when it was able to do so, nor that it intended to do so in the future. It was thus considered that extending the waiver had no impact on the potential market for this contract and so represented no material change.
- The change in discount levels is again detrimental to the providers and as such is not deemed a material change to the original contract.

This is useful stuff, but does not lay down specific criteria – there are none. So when considering making changes to existing contracts, take care not to set the new requirements outside the scope of the original contract as tendered and as laid down in the OJEU Notice.

What this means

> *Pressetext* is a very famous case and the principle it tested needs to be remembered as a potential area of grief. If it transpires that a provider of yours is giving a service that was not originally tendered you can be open to challenge

> Of course, if the circumstances change, as with Pressetext each case will have to be looked at on its own merits. However, as a general principle, the message regarding contract changes is writ large and clear. Don't do it.

> I have spoken of contract 'creep' and in long-term relationships this is a very real risk but, even with short-term arrangements, the temptation is there to ask a provider to do something maybe simply because they are already on site and able to do it. Such a move must be carefully considered: the risk attached to getting them to do a small task is minimal; if it is a large task, or the thin end of a wedge of requests, the risk increases rapidly

> In simple terms, you can only ask a contractor to do what was identified in the original Notice as being within the scope of the contract

> The solution? There are two options: [a] don't ask them to do it or [b] make sure the OJEU covers your requirements, and add maybe a bit of contingency in the scope, if you are able

Cases:

- *Pressetext Nachrichtenagentur GmbH v Republik Österreich (Bund), APA-OTS Originaltext – Service GmbH and APA Austria Presse Agentur registrierte Genossenschaft mit beschränkter Haftung , Case C-454/06; judgment of 19 June 2008.*

CHAPTER 6 – COLLUSION

What is collusion?

Collusion is where two or more parties work together in an endeavour to influence the outcome of a tender process. This is illegal. It is also a reason why, at all critical stages of a procurement, parties submitting PQQ or tender documents should *always* be asked to sign a declaration stating that they have not colluded with any party in the preparation of the tender.

Additionally, the Corporate Section of a Qualification Questionnaire should always ask if the Applicant has any past or current dealings or relationship with the client organisation or any person within the client organisation. It may be that they do have, in which case it needs to be a declared interest, and you will need to take a view on whether the relationship is too close for comfort and the Applicant discounted from the process.

Sometimes, when an interest is declared, so-called 'Chinese Walls' can be constructed to demonstrate a lack of collusion but you need to be certain of your position because a challenge by other bidders may need to be defended – can you *prove* the process was all fair and above-board?

In 2004, the EU delegated most of the authoritarian role to member states on a 'local' level[13], using their own legislation, so there is not a wealth of 'EU' cases to consider. In the UK, for example, the principle of fair tendering is laid down in The Competition Act of 1998 and many UK cases will hinge on that. In most cases the Office of Fair trading (OFT) will pursue the case. Of course, a bidder's collusion with an employee of the contracting authority may well come under the realms of the Bribery Act 2010 – bribery is a form of collusion – and we shall look at that Act in some detail later on.

Meanwhile, as part of the decentralisation process I mentioned above, it was laid down that there are three elements to consider

---

13. In this case 'local' means National – the home country.

with regards to a breach of Article 101 – the bit of the EU Regulations pertaining to competition:

- There must be some form of agreement, decision or concerted practice between the companies involved
- These agreements must be of the sort that might affect trade between EU member states
- Thus the agreement has as its object or effect the restriction, prevention or distortion of competition within the EU.

Let us look at an example from the UK.

Office of Fair Trading Investigation into the UK Construction Industry
The biggest example to hit the news in recent times was in 2009 when the Office of Fair Trading (OFT) found that 103 (so far as was known) construction companies had colluded in their tendering processes, breaching Chapter 1 of the 1998 Competition Act. Fines totalling over £129m were imposed for acts of collusive tendering between 2000 and 2006.

Breaches included:

a) the infamous 'scam' of 'cover pricing' – the act of putting in a price that will ensure 'competitors' win the contract whilst not appearing to be uninterested oneself, so maintaining good faith with the tendering authority - and
b) agreeing with fellow competitors the payment of compensation to them on the tenders you win

In other words, they 'divvied' up the work between them to the detriment of the competitive process and other poor bidders who were in the tendering process but not in their 'gang' or clique.

The whole mess caused a real stir, especially amongst Contracting Authorities who had contracts in full swing that had been won by those named in the OFT releases. The 'stir' was exacerbated by the fact that the OFT declared an amnesty, agreeing to reduce fines if firms owned up to the crime; on the back of this, several (if not many) of the implicated firms came forward and owned up to the practice. These confessions left no corners of doubt.

What this means

> Collusion is a serious issue and in law has connotations of fraud and bribery. As a procurement person, you can never know for sure that you have eliminated collusion. In practical terms, you can take steps that (a) make certain you have done all you can to prevent it and (b) demonstrate this as a fact should problems crop up later on, i.e. cover your back. I refer you back to the opening paragraphs of this chapter

> On a personal note, make sure you are never yourself put in a position where collusion – on any level – could be suspected and in terms of echoing this in your procurement practice, complete transparency is the key

> Disproving collusion can be very difficult

Cases:

- *OFT Press Release 135/09, 20th November 2009*

CHAPTER 7 – COMMUNITY BENEFITS

It's not as simple as we would like
This is an odd matter to consider because Community Benefits are seemingly innocent, but to include them as part of a tender evaluation model can transgress some key principles of EU procurement – and cause you a lot of trouble if you are not careful.

What are Community Benefits?
A community benefit is accepted as anything a contract can bring that is over and above the key objective of the contract (e.g. not just the building of a new school) which has a value to the community local to the contract or project. This value can be measured in cash (for example, a community chest or fund to which the contractor will contribute or even wholly support, or giving trade to local businesses) or kind (such as supporting local events or holding community fun days) or a combination of both or providing local employment and training opportunities.

It is incumbent on procurement professionals to extract as much value from a contract as possible, within the budget limitations, and this includes peripheral benefits such as those listed above. Some contracts, because of their nature, scope or value, do not offer much opportunity for such added value and reasonableness on the part of the tendering authority needs to hold sway, but some contracts – notably lengthy term contracts and partnering agreements – lend themselves admirably to bringing benefits to the community in which they serve and from where, in all honesty, contractors glean their profits.

Quite often, a successful approach can be to simply let the contractual relationship develop and let the benefits evolve from this relationship, but this is not wholly reliable (albeit perhaps cheaper, as the contractor may not have built in a provision for the benefits within their contract sum). My view is that the more direct approach is more honest and, in most cases, more effective. Most firms will respond positively under the right conditions – often they are very willing and experienced in this field - and full advantage should be taken of this predilection.

Of course, because regulations are involved, you cannot simply lay down community benefits as part of the tender requirements or you will transgress them, but there are ways and there is case law to help illustrate this.

Remember – the whole thrust of the EU Regulations and the Treaty on which they are based is freedom of movement across the EU and equality of opportunity to all in the tender process.

Gebroeders Beentjes v The Netherlands
This is a very famous case and is a good illustration of the points I have been discussing above. It was probably a real Road to Damascus moment when the EU recognised that procurement could be used to help realise social policies. This is strange, because in any organisation, procurement is at the forefront of advancing corporate aims and policies. Someone should have told them...

Anyway, Gebroeders Beentjes (Beentjes, as the case is known) failed to secure a contract, despite being the lowest-cost bidder, losing it instead to a company who agreed they could take on long-term unemployed people from the region to make up at least 70% of the required workforce. Beentjes said they were unable to meet this commitment.

Beentjes complained that this was an unlawful requirement but the ECJ found against the complaint on the grounds that they found the requirement:

a) Did not contravene EU Law and
b) Was a condition made clear in the OJEU Notice.

This was a landmark decision because other cases before and since have ruled similar community benefits requirements as illegal. So what was so special about Beentjes?

This is hard to answer – as I said at the beginning, there is a fine line between OK and not OK - so we'll look at a couple of other cases and try to gain a better view of how far we can go in specifying these community benefits.

Commission v Kingdom of Denmark

An example of an illegal requirement is the *Storebaelt*, where the stipulated requirement was to use, so far as possible, Danish materials, consumer goods, labour and equipment: not much scope for cross-border trading there. If you compare this with the client requirements of the *Beentjes* case, the degree of reasonableness is the key: The Netherlands required at least 70% (of whatever); *Storebaelt* wanted 100% of home-grown if they could get it. That was considered unreasonable and the court considered *"the Kingdom of Denmark failed to fulfil its obligations under Community law."*

European Communities v French Republic

A similar case, this time involving France, also decided that a requirement to employ local labour from a local project to try and reduce unemployment was lawful, so it seems there is a trend: essentially, requirements to boost local labour levels are good, but don't be greedy or unreasonable and make sure you include the requirement in the OJEU Notice.

All of a sudden, it seemed, some social benefits moved from being an operational performance issue into the realms of tender evaluation criteria. Just tread carefully: what the law will allow is still not clearly prescribed. It seems as if the procurement law world is waiting on more legal cases to help define the parameters – just make sure your procurement is not one of them.

Added Value

Life is strange. It is a fact that Added Value in a tender is a minefield.

The discussion above related to providing employment opportunities to the local population, but of course Added Value – community and other benefits beyond the immediate realms of the contract – extend far beyond that and the further beyond you get the more difficult and treacherous it becomes. The 'strange' part is how the Social Value Act 2013 pops up in the middle of it all, but we shall look at that Act specifically in Chapter 31. Meanwhile, I will look at Added Value in procurement in a more general context.

The problem with Added Value in a tender is that, if you ask bidders what added value they can offer, how do you evaluate it fairly and equitably across all bids? For example, taking a fairly naïve instance, you might simply ask bidders to 'describe in no more than 400 words what added value they can bring to the contract that will be of benefit to the local community.' Answers may range from a description of an elaborate scheme of apprenticeships and employment opportunities down to a simple 'none'.

Apart from any marks for honesty, the score for 'none' would be a simple zero, but scoring the elaborate offer against, say, an offer to establish a day centre for the elderly would be a whole different ball game. Beauty is in the eye of the beholder, and if you opt for the day centre, the provider of apprenticeships may well want to know on what basis the day centre scored – say – twice as many marks in the evaluation. It would be a sound point to raise and, if the score contributed to the tender outcome, would be worth a challenge (see Chapter 9 on Criteria). If the question scored no marks towards the evaluation, why ask it? Mr 'none' (above) is as likely to win the contract as any other bidder, despite offering nothing in terms of community benefits.

Considering all the above, then, the issues around seeking added value in a tender process is probably threefold:

1. The added value element you are looking for has to be stated in the OJEU Notice

2. It has to be related to the scope of the contract, not a random whim of the contracting authority
3. Undefined benefits are almost impossible to score without problems ensuing.

The advice is, unless you are able to legally seek added value that is relevant to the contract (and the answer to this is almost entirely and specifically instance-based) it is best to state that you expect added value or community benefits to come out of the relationship but leave it at that – let them develop.

One other approach is to explore a contractor's record of such benefits realised on previous contracts as part of the PQQ process. This can work, but once again the question of scoring apples v. pears arises. I have limited such questions to the number of employment / training / apprenticeship opportunities afforded in contracts and scored those against a clearly-stated formula.

This will help with the assessment of an Applicant firm and will also make it known what your expectations are, but always remember that some types of contract afford providers more opportunities than others – always be reasonable in your expectations.

What this means

> The *Beentjes* case opened some doors but did not solve all the problems of securing community benefits or added value as a contractual item assessed within a tender

> The creation of employment and training opportunities is always a favourite and is amongst the most easily secured, in legal terms at least, if not in reality.

> Essentially, beware of what you ask for and how you ask for it – the law has shown that some requirements can be included as part of a tender but the headline clue here is that they cannot be included if they introduce any lack of equality of opportunity

> *– all* the bidders have to be in a position[14] to provide what is wanted

> If the requirements are part of an evaluation model, my alarm bell would ring, as it may not be possible to safely assess one proposal (essentially an item of added value) as being better than another. Promises of often intangible benefits are easy to make and sometimes difficult to secure in practice, so beware of that

> Proportionality is relevant: do not ask for more than the contract could reasonably be expected to provide (which, in fact, might be nothing), even though the Social Value Act may require you to consider the possibilities, and remember that your requirements need to be relevant to the nature of the contract or service

> My view is that it is better to indicate that it is expected that some social benefits will emanate from the contract, but let them develop as the relationship grows and remember: contractors are often better at this than we are

Cases:

- *Gebroeders Beentjes BV v State of the Netherlands. [1988] EUECJ R-31/87 (20 September 1988)*
- Commission v Kingdom of Denmark *[1993] EUECJ C-243/89 (22 June 1993)*
- *European Communities v French Republic [2000] EUECJ C-225/89 (26 September 2000)*

---

14. 'In a position' in procurement equality terms, that is, meaning that some bidders must not be specifically disadvantaged by the requirement and it must *not* be anything that contravenes cross-border trading and working rights.

CHAPTER 8 – COMPETITION

What is Competition?

This seems an obvious question, but it is a touchy subject in EU-procurement land. Competition – specifically open and fair competition – is fundamental to the whole ethos of EU Procurement legislation and is laid down in the EU Treaty on which these Regulations are based. *And* this competition has to extend fairly across the whole of the EU territories. That's some competition.

Referring you back to the chapter on collusion (which, of course, is contrary to fair competition) I stated that when it comes down to issues of fair competition, the law reverts to the homeland for justice to be done. That means that transgressions in the UK come under UK law and that is a pity for some because the UK laws on competition are amongst the harshest anywhere.

In the UK, the legal regime is defined by two pieces of legislation – The Competition Act of 1998 and The Enterprise Act of 2002 – and the prime enforcer of this legislation is the Office of Fair Trading (OFT). They starred in the case of Cover Pricing in the construction industry, which headlined Chapter 6 on collusion.

A close link between the OFT and EU Procurement processes is maintained through the OFT maintaining a close working relationship with the EU Commission (amongst others), and this ties in with breaches of EU Competition Law being dealt with 'at home'. In other words, the OFT deals with cases in the UK of infringements of EU Regulations that relate to fair competition[15].

The name 'Office of Fair Trading' does not have the foreboding aura that some other agencies' names might have, but their powers are formidable. The OFT can:

---

15. The Office of Fair trading (OFT) also rules on the impact on market competitiveness of mergers. This role is often in the news but is of no interest to us here.

- Carry out unannounced on-the-spot investigations ('dawn raids')
- Enter and search premises
- Impose measures to immediately halt behaviour they believe to be uncompetitive
- Impose fines - but no ordinary fines – these can be up to 10% of a company's previous year's annual, worldwide turnover in magnitude!
- Order companies party to an infringement to cease their corrupt activities forthwith
- Accept a commitment to abstain from uncompetitive behaviour

And to add to this, their powers have legal backing. That's some 'Office'. We can look at some examples.

Office of Fair Trading and Digifly Europe SRL
Digifly, an Italian firm, made hang-gliding variometers and had an exclusive agreement with Snowdon Gliders as its UK agent.

The Agreement contained the clause: *"The importer is free in prices and conditions management, but in any case, the final prices of contractual products shall not be lower than those granted by the producer."* It was considered that this clause set a minimum price for the product, which is in breach of what is known as the 'Chapter 1 prohibition'.

Looking back at the powers of the Office of Fair Trading (OFT), the parties assured the OFT (commitment) that the clause had never been and would never be invoked but in addition amended the clause to read: *"The general importer is free in prices and conditions management"*. Problem solved.

This Chapter 1 prohibition applies to an agreement (which does not have to be written but could be merely an act of collusion) between two parties to work contrary to the interest of (appreciable) competition within the UK.

There is also a Chapter 2, which applies where an organisation in a position of market dominance uses this power to the detriment of competition in the UK.

Not all cases go before the OFT: if the issue is one that has gone through the courts of claim and counterclaim, for example, the courts will make decisions based on competition and EU law.

Here is an interesting example:

Bernard Crehan v Inntrepreneur Pub Company Limited and Brewman Group Limited
In 1991, Bernard Crehan (Crehan) took on leases for two pubs from Inntrepreneur Pub Company Limited (IPCL) and the agreement included 'ties' that required him to buy his beer from Courage. The business failed and Crehan was left with money owing to Courage and IPLC and was sued by them for the debts. The case went to the High Court.

Crehan claimed as a defence that he had to buy beer from Courage and that this was unlawful, being in breach of Article 81 of the EU Treaty[16]. He also used this as a counterclaim in that he was forced to buy beer at prices higher than he would have paid elsewhere and that this contributed to his business' failure.

As part of the decision-making process, the ECJ was consulted on whether a party in a case under Article 81 could claim damages and, in a nutshell, it was agreed it could but not to the point where it could interfere with a court of the land precluding a party who has 'significant responsibility' for the distortion of competition exacting damages. In other words, the English Court can take into account any element of bullying by a monopoly or similar and react accordingly.

Article 81 was a part of the EU Treaty of 1981 that prohibited any agreement that inhibits trade and/or competition between

16. Since replaced by Articles 101 and 102 of the TFEU – the Treaty on the Functioning of the European Union

member states and which allows decisions to be made at national level. Enough said: back to the case...

The High Court held that the 'tie' did not infringe Article 81 so the Crehan claim failed. The Court considered that the 'tie' did not restrict other beer manufacturers from entering the market (despite the fact they could not enter Mr Crehan's market, of course, but this is an EU Article). The Court also made two interesting points:

1. They would not take into account a similar case involving Whitbread, where an infringement of Article 81 *was* considered to have taken place (!) and
2. Had the 'tie' been an infringement of Article 81, Crehan's claim for damages would have been upheld because the conditions would certainly have been seen to contribute to the demise of Mr Crehan's business. As it was, they didn't, or so the Court held and, on this basis, they awarded damages, but limited them to the value of loss of profits from the date the business closed to the date of the judgement and nothing more.

An interesting twist. So, of course, there was an appeal.

Crehan lodged an appeal.

The Court of Appeal held in Crehan's favour! More than that, they criticised the High Court for forming their own opinion rather than taking into account the findings of the Whitbread case (which was an EU Commission Case). The Court of Appeal, in other words, felt that the instance of IPLC was not considered in the light of the EU's approach to competition. Further than that, they felt the Agreement Crehan had signed with IPLC *did* contribute to the foreclosure and in fact cited another case (*Delimitis v Henninger Brau*) as an example of where the network was smaller than the IPCL one and yet had still contributed to business failures.

With regards to damages, on this revised view of the monopoly situation (for that is what it was), they instead awarded all losses assessed from the date of the demise of the business.

IPCL appealed (it seems it was their turn) and this meant it had to go to the highest court in the land – the House of Lords. This is where it got complicated.

The House of Lords overturned the Appeal Court's decision. Strange as it may seem, they considered that the High Court decision, in not following the EU Commission's Whitbread decision when considering the Courage one did not present a conflict. They considered that the Crehan case could only be guided by the EU Commission decision if the outcome were to be decided by the EU Commission. Because the Commission made a decision about an issue with different parties, the House of Lords considered the precedent did not apply.

Further to this decision, and to reinforce the point, the House of Lords maintained that there is no EU Rule requiring a National Court to follow an ECJ[17] decision where they are deciding on a case other than one between the parties before the ECJ. In other words, they would have to uphold an ECJ decision but, as a National Court, they do not have to consider any decision by the ECJ as a precedent in national law.

Complicated stuff, this competition law – and very unpredictable.

What this means

> As my closing comment above relates, competition law is a minefield all of its own. So far as procurement is concerned, you must ensure equality of opportunity (so as not to stifle competition) and transparency (to demonstrate equality of opportunity)

---

17. ECJ – European Court of Justice

> I think the key point to remember is that, even with below-threshold tenders, the values of the EU Treaty apply – and apply in law. The Treaty requires: competition, equality of opportunity, transparency and proportionality. Breach these and your tender may not be considered competitive in the context of the relevant legislation

> There is, of course, a link between competition (or lack of it) and collusion but I will leave you to think on that

---

Cases:

- *Office of Fair Trading (OFT) and Digifly Europe SRL – Press Release 7th July 2003*
- *Bernard Crehan v Inntrepreneur Pub Company Limited and Brewman Group Limited [2003] EWHC 1510 (Ch), judgment of 26 June 2003.*
- *Delimitis v Henninger Brau Case C-233/89 [1991] ECR I-935*

CHAPTER 9 – CRITERIA

What is it about Criteria?

If you have read the preceding chapters you will have noticed a common theme, or rather, themes: timescales and criteria. The reason is simple. Firstly, those of you who understand procurement (which I assume is all who would read a book like this) will know that the thing that primarily sets EU procurements aside from any non-EU procurement is the obsession with timescales. Most of the regulations are aimed at ensuring transparency, free movement of trade and all the other 'stuff' laid down in the EU Treaty of 1991[18], but the importance of timescales is up there in the vanguard position and often in quite a complex manner (see Chapter 4 on Challenges and Out of Time, for example).

In terms of criteria (that is, both PQQ and tender evaluation criteria), the EU is quite emphatic but again in the sense of transparency: say what you are going to do at the time of OJEU and then do it. Quite simple, everyone thought. Then along came 2008 and Letting International and the procurement world went into a flat spin. If truth be known, it is only now starting to calm down, but the legal profession is still busy...

So, looking at criteria, what *is* all the fuss about? In simple terms, the EU says that the way a tender (or a PQQ) is to be assessed has to be declared and you cannot deviate from this methodology – at all. The OJEU Notice provides space for publishing the criteria, or you can lay them down in the issued documentation, but whichever way you do it there are three cardinal rules:

1. You must make clear how you will evaluate the submissions
2. You must stick to that
3. You must declare *all* criteria and sub-criteria, and so on (see Mermec UK Ltd v Network Rail Infrastructure Ltd in Chapter 4).

---

18. Plus amendments, of course.

It sounds simple, but many, many cases reach court because bidders or applicants believe the criteria have not been applied as they were told they would be. Sometimes they are right. Make sure that doesn't happen to you.

A natural response is that, if you need to change the criteria or evaluation methodology, you can issue a clarification to all parties. An option is to issue an amendment to the OJEU Notice, and this is the legally safer option: it is clear and precise but is more of a task or process than simply issuing a clarification and this deters people. Normally, an Amendment is issued when the changes are fairly major; if they are not thought to be too serious or drastic, a clarification is often considered adequate.

A clarification during the actual process (i.e. during the period of PQQ or tender return) is much less reliable as case law (including some of the examples in this book) will reveal (see *Lianakis,* below). Sometimes a 'clarification' is accused of muddying the waters or otherwise disadvantaging participants; sometimes it is proposed that: 'if the revised evaluation methodology had been declared in the OJEU Notice, other bidders may have taken an interest in the process.' This postulation can be real or verging on fantasy (depending on the degree of change), but it can be hard to argue against such a claim. In either case, you could be in breach of EU Law.

It's always best, of course, to get it right before you go out to OJEU, and remember:

- You do not need any great detail at time of OJEU
- You need full and proper details of the PQQ evaluation process with the PQQ documentation
- You need full and proper details of the tender evaluation process with the tender documentation
- Neither the PQQ nor the tender evaluation methodology may vary from the information given out as part of the process.

By way of illustration and, I hope, as a guide on how you might proceed so as to avoid such problems (the key purpose of this book, after all), I will look at a few cases selected on the basis of impact, interest and validity. They are discussed in no particular order.

Letting International Ltd v London Borough of Newham
Whilst I did say I was not going to set the cases out in any particular order, this case (which happens to come first) was a seminal legal action that caused a monumental stir amongst procurement professionals everywhere. The interesting thing is that the London Borough of Newham (Newham) got picked up (if that is the right phrase) on something that had, until then, been pretty much general practice all over the place, and this despite the *Lianakis* case which had preceded it (see later).

The case concerns the tendering, by Newham, of two Frameworks to provide various services for private sector leased properties. Letting International Ltd (Letting) went forward to the tender list and the ITT explained that the tender would be evaluated against *MEAT* criteria comprising:

- Compliance with the specification - 50%
- Price - 40%
- Premises and staffing details - 10%

Letting were not successful in their bid and, after some correspondence, Letting considered that Newham had not, contrary to the EU Regulations, acted in a fair and transparent manner in its evaluation of the bids.

Proceedings reached the High Court on 27th November 2008, where Letting alleged:

- Newham had used five sub-criteria (themselves further divided) to which different weightings were applied and yet none of these were declared in the tender documents, breaching the requirement for transparency

- The marking model Newham used only awarded the maximum of five marks available if the submission exceeded the requirements of the specification. It was not stated in the documentation that 'simply' meeting the specification would not yield maximum marks. Again, transparency was the issue
- Newham made many plain errors in assessing Letting's bid, resulting in an unfair and non-objective assessment.

Setting aside some of the legal and other wrangles that ensued, Letting managed to secure an injunction forbidding Newham from awarding any contracts under the Frameworks until the matter had been resolved.

Newham countered that it was not obliged to declare all aspects of its evaluation process down to the finest detail and the Court referred back to a recent case (*Lianakis*, which, counter-intuitively, we shall look at next) where the ECJ had ruled that:

- The Contracting Authority has, in the interests of transparency, to declare the criteria it is going to use in its evaluation process and bidders should, therefore, be aware of all the criteria that are to be used so that they can best prepare their tenders.
- Similarly, a Contracting Authority cannot apply weightings that it has not already declared to bidders. All bidders have to be treated fairly so all bidders need to know (equally) of the weighting being applied.

Letting maintained that, had they known of the 'additional' criteria and the way weightings were going to be applied, they would have prepared their bid in a different manner to better present their offer to the Contracting Authority (my wording – but remember this point).

Newham contested this claim by Letting, but the Court rejected Newham's argument and instead pointed out that to say a bidder would or would not have prepared a tender differently 'had they known' is not relevant[19] – a breach is a breach regardless or not of whether a different bid would have ensued had the criteria been properly declared. Nevertheless (and perhaps inconsequentially), the Court acknowledged that 'proper' disclosure by Newham would have resulted in a differently-prepared bid.

Of particular interest – and something that crops up often when preparing evaluation criteria – is that Newham argued that the so-called sub-criteria (my terminology) were not sub-criteria at all but merely a marking mechanism (in other words, a guide to bid assessors). The Court also rejected this saying, basically, that if something is an aspect against which a tender is assessed then it is a criterion (and so, therefore, should be declared).

In terms of errors (a relatively minor point in the context of this chapter), whilst the Court did not agree with Letting's claim *per se,* it did find other errors in the evaluation that had scored Letting too low and the winning bid too high, although no deliberate collusion was either claimed or implied (Letting was, in fact, already an existing provider to Newham).

Newham levelled another argument at Letting's claims, saying that Letting had failed to demonstrate that, had Newham not committed any of the alleged infringements, they would have won a contract. In other words, Letting had failed to identify any actual loss. The Court rejected that argument, too (it was not Newham's best day), saying that – again – the fact that Letting did not suffer any actual loss did not mean they could not justifiably raise a challenge; all Letting had to do was show that they had been impaired from winning the contract: that is, their chances had been made worse.

At this point it should be noted that there is no pre-condition to the commencement of proceedings. The Court has made this clear twice, now. The principle applied is that any lack of transparency

---

19. An interesting point because it will be seen that, in other circumstances, the instance 'had they known…' would be a vital consideration. However, this is a clear and simple case of a breach of the regulations (if there is such a thing).

or fairness (as per the EU Treaty) is an infringement and any loss of chance of winning (i.e. any unevenness in the playing field) represents grounds for a claim.

Another (yes – yet another) interesting aspect of this case is that, at the end of it all, the High Court 'suggested' that the two parties might agree on a mutually satisfactory remedy to the situation, bearing in mind the outcome of the case (Newham lost on all counts). The High Court went even further and 'suggested' that Newham might just add Letting to the Framework.

And so it was.

My personal view is that this 'remedy' was an odd one for the court to propose and in principle had the potential to lead to problems later on, on all sorts of counts, including:

- The Contracting Authority being caused to have more parties to a Framework than they had declared in the OJEU Notice
- The parties originally awarded to the Framework would have their potential return from it diluted by the addition of another provider – and could this lead to potential claims for loss of profit?
- Newham may have opted not to award any work to Letting, so negating the purpose of the judge's recommendation - and could *this* have led to a further claim from Letting?

In reality, no remedy would have been ideal or obvious to all parties so I shall pursue this angle no further, save to refer you to *McLaughlin & Harvey Ltd v Department of Finance & Personnel* at the end of this chapter.

This has been a relatively long account but the repercussions of this judgement have been far reaching – more so than *Lianakis*, for some reason (see next case). There are few cases (at least in procurement) that have had such a major impact on practice. As I said at the beginning of the chapter, Newham were probably doing, in many ways, what countless other Contracting Authorities had been doing all over the place.

'Everyone' had to take stock and carefully review the way they formulated their documentation and exercised their evaluations. All of a sudden, Contracting Authorities had to explain in considerable detail how they were going to score a submission, to the point of explaining marks not just against criteria but against sub-criteria (and sub-sub criteria, remember) as well, and all this without actually giving bidders the answer. They (we) found it hard, but it is possible.

How to draw up an evaluation or scoring model in light of all this is too involved a topic to go into here (that is not this book's purpose) so you will need to refer elsewhere for the solution, but the lesson is there to be learned and, of equal importance, the profile of the case was such that bidders are now much more aware of this requirement and as a result the risk of challenge is all the greater. So remember – make sure it is clear to bidders exactly how you are going to score their submission: do not have scores or criteria which you have not told them about, and show them how the scores are related to the criteria against which the submission is to be judged. No secrets.

An aside point: I said earlier to remember a point. You probably haven't, but it was with regards to bidders preparing a different bid "had they known...," etc., etc.). This 'test' of due process crops up repeatedly as it is actually at the heart of the principles of openness and fairness (two EU Treaty basics). I will pop two examples in now, just because I think it is of interest and hopefully may be of some assistance.

There are two key instances when the question "had they known..." should be asked:

1. When considering if you have declared the evaluation criteria as you ought. At feedback, could they come back to you and say

'You did not tell us that; had we *known*...etc.'? If they could, you need to be clearer.

2. When considering adding to or changing a contract later in its life. Contracts will grow and develop but there comes a point where the EU will say: 'This is a different contract, and it should have been tendered' (see Chapter 5). There are no rules on this[20] – like with so many things in procurement you fly this one by the seat of your pants – but you have to ask the question whether, had the changed requirements been in the original contract (the changes can be specification, volume, scope – anything) would the bidders have had cause to change their submission? If the answer is 'yes', the EU will probably think you ought to have tendered the changes. Of course, 'they' might never know, but a firm who wanted the work might, and so it begins. They will have the right to challenge the variation on the basis of the EU Regulations. Your choice – a consideration of risk - but I cannot advocate any breach of the regulations – and neither should you.

So, for (2) above, make sure you stick to what was advertised in the OJEU Notice and make sure the OJEU Notice, so far as it can, covers what the contract can foreseeably be required to cover, maybe plus a bit.

Back to the business of this chapter. Let's look at *Lianakis*.

Emm.G. Lianakis AE and others v Dimos Alexandroupolis and others
The Judge in the Letting case above referred to the Lianakis interpretation. This is it and it is interesting because [a] it illustrates the difference between evaluation at the PQQ and the tender stages and [b] the ECJ arrived at its decision whilst considering matters it had not originally been asked about. I guess people do get distracted...

---

20. There are references in the Regulations to increasing the value by more than 15%, and this is picked up in the new 2014 Directive, but that is one aspect amongst several that need to be considered.

The tender in question concerned some town planning projects by the Municipal Council of Alexandroupolis (MCA). The evaluation criteria set out in the OJEU Notice comprised:

- Proven experience on projects over the last three years
- Manpower and equipment, and
- Ability to complete on time, commitment and professional potential.

During the evaluation process (note the timing), MCA further defined the criteria and set weightings of 60%, 20% and 30% for the three aspects respectively. Additionally, it stated that the first point would be assessed on the value of the projects worked on and would also consider numbers of employees and value of work previously carried out.

Two losing consortia challenged the outcome of the tender, claiming that the award was based on criteria announced by the Council subsequent to the OJEU and the tender documents.

The Greek Court raised a question with the ECJ on whether, within the Regulations, a contract authority could evaluate a bid on the basis of criteria set during the evaluation process. Of course, we now know they cannot, but that is only because of the precedents we are looking at here; so the ECJ had to make some deliberations, and they took an interesting view.

First of all they considered whether the evaluation criteria chosen by the authority were right in the first place and came to the conclusion that consideration of a bidder's experience, manpower, equipment and ability to complete work to deadlines were all factors that ought to be considered at PQQ stage. This is because, within the Regulations, pre-selection is to assess the ability of service providers to perform the required services, particularly with regard to their skills, capacity, financial standing, experience and reliability. In other words, the PQQ stage has to look back, and a firm's capability and capacity cannot be used as tender award criteria.

The Regulations go on to say that the tender itself has to be evaluated on the basis of lowest price or most economically advantageous tender (MEAT)[21] and nothing else. In other words, the tender evaluation has to look forwards to the contract itself and the bidder's proposals to meet its requirements, and it has to assess these proposals against the criteria laid out in either the Contract Notice or the issued tender documents.

The first thing they decided, then, was that the criteria the contracting authority (MCA) had laid down should not have been used to evaluate the tender submissions in the first place. To me, that is quite a major transgression.

They then got round to answering the question they had been asked.

They considered the question from the aspect of transparency and the key issue at hand is always: was the action such that

- the declared criteria were not altered
- the changes, even if known earlier, would not have affected the preparation of the bids[22]
- there was no discrimination against any of the bidders.

The ECJ concluded that, because the weightings and additional (sub) criteria were decided after the bids were submitted, the action they took did not meet the acid test of transparency and equal treatment.

I have laid down above three little 'tests' that the ECJ considered: they are related here purely to show the train of logic. Please do *not* try to be clever and use these criteria to do things you shouldn't! Learn the lesson: *Lianakis* and *Letting* set out what we now take for granted: make all your evaluation criteria clear at the outset and do not change them. You will then be safe – I hope.

---

21. MEAT – a balanced evaluation of price and quality criteria.
22. Note this in the light of the views expressed on this matter in the case of Letting International v. London Borough of Newham and my comments which followed, i.e. "Had they known…"

Healthcare At Home Ltd v The Common Services Agency

This is one from Scotland and I have included it here on three counts: (a) it is a more recent example of issues around evaluation criteria and (b) it is one where the challenge did not succeed, in contrast to the two other cases I have covered so far and (c) it raised some fairly common types of challenges and some interesting court decisions.

For those who do not know, The Common Services Agency (CSA) is the NHS in Scotland and it issued ITTs for the provision of various medical services including nursing administration and support and the dispensing and distribution of a particular drug (Tastuzumab).

The tenders were to be evaluated against MEAT criteria comprising:

- Quality of Service – 35%
- Risk and Deliverability – 25%
- Price – 20%
- Nursing Support – 10%
- Patient Support – 5%
- Transport – 5%

Each of these main criteria was in turn divided into sub-criteria and the weightings allocated to each of these were given in the ITT documentation. So far so good.

Healthcare At Home Ltd (HAH) were the incumbent and submitted a tender. After the evaluation, they were advised that they had been unsuccessful and that BUPA Home Healthcare (BUPA) had been successful.

HAH lodged a complaint and issued a legal challenge alleging infringement of the need for transparency and equal treatment due to:

a) the lack of clarity in the award criteria
b) the evaluation of bids against those criteria and

c) a failure to provide adequate reasons (i.e. lack of information during Alcatel).

The judgement was long and involved and I shall not dwell on all of it but I shall cherry-pick what I believe to be the main points of interest – and the bits most likely to be of use to you.

The court laid down a long and interesting list of items that could be used to define transparency, equal treatment and transparency, and these included:

- The contracting authority must ensure that the evaluation criteria it chooses are not discriminatory and they must be applied objectively and equally to all bidders

- It must be assured that bidders (or Applicants at PQQ stage) are in 'equal positions' when they put together their submissions, i.e. no bidder can have any advantage over any other so far as the information issued by the Contracting Authority is concerned.

- These criteria cannot be altered and the evaluation cannot consider things not declared which, had they been made known at time of tender, would have caused the bidders to change their submission (there it is again – the principle that keeps cropping up).

- Any criteria which assess a bidder's ability or capacity to carry out the contract are *selection* criteria (i.e. for PQQ stage) and are not to be used as tender evaluation criteria, which are to look forwards at the proposed performance of the contract itself.

- No criterion can be so vague as to give the evaluator scope to award a contract as they wish rather than strictly through evaluation against the declared criteria.

- An evaluation process can allow no margin of interpretation regarding how rigidly it will interpret the requirements of the Regulations with respect to equality, transparency and non-discrimination but the process *can* have leeway in its judgement or assessment of how well bidders have met the criteria. Material errors can be challenged but an evaluation panel's views on a bidder's proposal, generally, cannot be.

Some of these points are already known, but a couple of them look at the issues from a slightly different angle, especially the last one. But still, care is needed to ensure that any latitude in an evaluation does not go so far as to be outside the declared criteria. This has to be a matter of judgement, but the principle expressed by the Court is a point that can be made clear to an Evaluation Panel, members of which can sometimes be a little unsure of how their views will stand up to scrutiny.

A discussion ensued because HAH had maintained that the documentation was unclear and that bidders could have interpreted the evaluation criteria in different ways, thus transgressing the requirement for transparency and equal treatment. Presumably, they felt that those who interpreted it correctly were the lucky ones and had an unfair advantage. The Court's response was interesting.

The Court held that to require an Authority to explain or direct to a degree that ensured all bidders would arrive at precisely the same conclusion would be an impractical and burdensome demand. But it went further than that, going so far as to say that such an outcome would only serve to stifle the bidders' initiative and experience and perhaps even quell innovative solutions to the requirement.

The observation made by the Court was that it would be in order for a Contracting Authority to expect a tenderer to use reasonable judgement and insight to understand what a criterion or sub-criterion encompasses. Thus, where an accusation (or challenge) of undisclosure is levelled, the Court could ask whether the matter claimed as being undeclared would have been considered as included by a reasonably well-informed and diligent bidder. I presume the corollary is that a Contracting Authority can expect such diligence of its bidders, but for safety's sake I would not make too many such assumptions in your tenders.

Another interesting decision came with regards to the HAH claim that feedback was not sufficiently clear. HAH had maintained that CSA had not adequately or consistently explained why the HAH responses had not been as good as those provided by BUPA and so had received lower scores. On this point, the Court maintained that the feedback by CSA had been sufficiently clear to allow HAH to articulate its grievance and bring the challenge, so this claim was also discounted! This surprised me – but it was an interesting take on the matter, I thought.

There is a lot more to this case, and it is worth a look, but it is not all relevant to what we are looking at in this chapter.

One last case on this topic, this time looking at the evaluation of sub-conscious criteria. Who could resist? Also, it's interesting how the same names keep cropping up...

Lancashire v Environmental Waste Controls Ltd
The contract tendered was for the provision of 23 waste recycling sites in the Greater Manchester Area. The contract was won by SITA, despite the fact that Environmental Waste Controls Ltd (EWC) submitted a lower price bid (by quite a margin) and so EWC challenged the decision.

The contention by EWC was that, in reaching its evaluation decision, Lancashire had – albeit subconsciously – taken into account (a) EWC's less than favourable financial position (although EWC had to have passed the PQQ stage – so how did that happen?) and (b) the fact that they had submitted a considerably cheaper bid than their competitors (see Chapter 25 on Suicide Bids).

The High Court found in favour of EWC and agreed that the Council had, indeed, subconsciously considered these factors during the assessment. Funnily enough, the High Court also acknowledged the fact that Lancashire had intentionally *tried* to avoid taking into account both EWC's financial standing and their low bid but they had, nonetheless, let it influence their evaluation. The High Court also confirmed they had no suspicion that the assessments had been deliberately manipulated. They nevertheless found in favour of EWC on the basis of 'subconscious' considerations.

Lancashire were adamant they had not been influenced by the extraneous factors and Appealed.

The Court of Appeal accepted that evaluators could, indeed, be influenced by subconscious factors, but this had failed to be proven in this particular case. In reaching this decision, they considered how the evaluator came across whilst giving evidence – he had taken early advice on the matter of considering EWC's financial standing prior to making the evaluation. The Appeal Court therefore felt it was inappropriate (my wording) to adjudge that the evaluation had not been undertaken on the basis of the facts of the submission.

All that can be expected of the evaluator is that they embark upon the process with the deliberate intention of considering only the relevant evidence in front of them. For the High Court to consider otherwise would not have been correct – in fact, the Appeal Court considered it was unlawful to do so.

Thus the Court of Appeal rejected the original decision and upheld Lancashire's appeal, stating that they did not consider that the evaluation of sub-conscious criteria had taken place.

You will note they did not rule out the fact that it could happen in other instances, though...

McLaughlin & Harvey Ltd v Department of Finance & Personnel
This is just a quick follow-up to the Letting International case, where I discussed the court's remedy in some detail, primarily because the court 'suggested' the successful claimant be added

to the Framework rather than nullify the Framework or award damages. In this case, the Court opted to set aside the Framework in its entirety so I thought we should look at it. The arguments are interesting.

The procurement, by the Northern Irish Department of Finance and Personnel (DFP), was to set up five contractors to lead on construction projects over the life of a Framework, with awards to be made via mini-competition. McLaughlin & Harvey (MH) came sixth, but with a score within 1% of bidders placed 4th and 5th.

At debriefing, MH learned that the evaluation method used did not coincide with that declared at time of tender (precise details not critical here) and the court – after consideration of the Letting and the Lianakis cases - found in their favour. Incidentally, they criticised DFP for not having adequate notes relating to the evaluation process, so be warned.

MH had requested that either they be added to the Framework (as in Letting International) or the Framework Agreement be set aside.

The Court noted that its actions are somewhat limited once a contract has been awarded (see Remedies Directive) but the only 'award' that had taken place was ostensibly that of the Framework Agreement. The court was at pains to point out that a Framework Agreement is not the same as a contract and that the Regulations themselves go to lengths to distinguish between the two.

On this basis it decided it was the better option to set aside the Framework, despite DFP's objections, and I shall relate the reasoning because a lot of it coincides with my own considerations of the court's decision in the *Letting* case (yes – that one again!).

The court reasoned:

- The risk of litigation from the other bidders was minimal. They would have to re-bid, but this time as part of a process that would be more open and transparent. If they were genuinely the best, they would win again. Not much sympathy there, then!

- Adding a sixth member to a Framework that had been 'designed' for five and which the members had assumed would comprise five would 'dilute' the opportunities for the original five and potentially lead to litigation. A retender would result in greater fairness than this solution presented.

- The court also stated there was no legal precedent for enforcing the adding of a firm to a Framework – remember in the case of Letting, the judge merely 'suggested' it.

- Damages would be hard to assess and, whilst this remained a possible course of action, it would be less fair than re-running the competition.

- An interesting last point – the evaluation process – judged as inadequate - did not necessarily secure the best five bidders to the Framework, which is the duty inherent in a public procurement (whether or not the best five would include MH was not considered relevant). The court added that it would be an additional waste of funds to pay a contractor for a project *and* pay another firm compensation in the form of damages for not being included in the tender (i.e. mini-competition) process.

The above is an interesting commentary: it notes the lack of a contractor's level of security in their award to a Framework Agreement when compared with that of the award of a proper Contract (even one emanating from a Framework): a 'proper' contract could not have been set aside under the circumstances. The court also made light of the risk of challenge from disgruntled other bidders who, until the judgement, thought they had been successfully appointed to a Framework.

I do not know if any other litigation did arise from the decision (in law, DRP could well have been liable through faulty process) but the procurement costs must have been considerable and similar sums would have had to have been expended in the event of a re-run – that is assuming the Framework was retendered.

What this means

> Make sure you declare *all* the criteria you are going to use to evaluate a submission, and the scores attached to them

> Making your quality submission requirements clear without giving the answer is difficult, but it is possible, nevertheless...

> The court expects bidders to be able to interpret tendering requirements – the key is that they must not be ambiguous

> Maintain the distinction between retrospective criteria which look at capability and capacity and are assessed at the PQQ stage and the criteria for assessing forward-looking proposals for the contract

And an aside...

> When considering price:quality split for a *MEAT*[23] evaluation, test the model carefully because sometimes, if the split is wrong, either one or the other (normally quality) will be unable to influence the outcome, no matter how high its score. In other words, a *MEAT* evaluation might still end up a lowest-price award, no matter how good the quality score

---

Cases:

- *Letting International Ltd v London Borough of Newham [2008] EWHC 1583 (QB), judgment of 7 July 2008*
- *Emm.G. Lianakis AE and others v Dimos Alexandroupolis and others [2008]ECJ Case C-532/06 judgment of 24 January 2008*
- *Healthcare At Home Ltd v The Common Services Agency [2012] ScotCS CSOH_75 (01 May 2012)*

23. MEAT – Most Economically Advantageous Tender balancing cost and quality scores to reach an outcome.

- *Lancashire County Council v Environmental Waste Controls Ltd [2010] EWCA Civ 1381, judgment of 7 December 2010*
- *McLaughlin & Harvey Ltd v Department of Finance & Personnel, judgment on remedies, 30 October 2008 ([2008] NIQB 122)*

CHAPTER 10 – DEVELOPMENT & LAND DEALS

What about Development?

Development is included, obversely, because land deals are exempt from the EU Regulations, but between Development Agreements, Public Works Contracts and Land Deals lie very muddy waters. Things are not always what they seem, so it is always good to double check, and as a result, 'test' cases are often brought to court. We shall look at some cases now to try and get some clarity. Here's hoping.

First of all, when is a public works contract not a public works contract?

Jean Auroux and Others v Commune de Roanne

Known as the Roanne Case, this all started in 2002 when the Municipal Council of Roanne (Roanne) authorised the mayor to enter into contract with the Société d'Equipement du Département de la Loire (SEDL) to build a leisure centre in the town.

The name of the intended constructor shows them to be a semi-public (therefore part municipal) organisation but the matter of contracting to 'internal' bodies is a major issue in its own right which we shall consider elsewhere in this book (see Chapter 18). For now, we are interested in the matter of tendering development opportunities and/or land deals so shall consider this aspect for the moment.

The contract involved obtaining the land and constructing car parking and public spaces for Roanne Council, along with various other leisure amenities (cinema, leisure centre, etc.) which would all be sold off. SEDL were to project manage the exercise and they would outsource all the construction work (through EU compliant tender processes) and Roanne would part-fund the project and underwrite all liabilities.

Jean Aroux claimed that the project was a major works contract and should have been put out to open tender. Roanne countered that the 'contract' was a 'public development agreement' between two public bodies, and so exempt from the EU Regulations. Roanne supported their argument by pointing out that SEDL was a contracting body (i.e. going to tender the work out and so exempt from EU tendering requirements), their contract was for project management services and not works and anyway, very little of the development benefits reverted to Roanne.

In other words, it was advocated that the works were in the public interest and no profits were arising, so it was a public works contract, came under the public works directive and so was exempt from the regulations, particularly insofar as the threshold for public works contracts would not be exceeded.

The ECJ, however, were having none of it. They stated that the prime purpose of the exercise was for the provision of public works construction services carried out to the requirements of Roanne and that the work SEDL was doing was 'merely' (my word) preparatory to this. In more precise detail the court laid down:

- A construction contract does not, by definition, have to be solely for the use of a public body or be in the public interest for it to be defined as a public works contract
- Public works contracts can be carried out on land not owned by the contracting authority
- When defining a contract, where there are multiple elements (i.e. a mixture of works, services and supplies), the main purpose of the exercise has to define the nature of the contract (a point which applies in other circumstances such as works/ services)
- When looking at financial values and thresholds, the entire financial consideration has to be taken into account – not just monies coming from the public body (in the Roanne case, the proceeds from the sell-off of the leisure facilities, for example).
- SEDL could have awarded contracts below the EU threshold

and also were not under the direct control of Roanne so in no way could the arrangement be considered as an 'in-house' contract.

Aroux won the day and this caused concerns that, even if the Authority's involvement in a development project is fairly remote, the 'land deal' would still require an EU procurement process regardless of whether:

- The authority would own any of the developed assets
- The work would be sub-contracted by the developer and
- Any sub-contract work would be tendered in line with the EU Procurement Regulations

All of a sudden, regeneration projects all over the UK were put on hold but luckily *Helmut Muller* came to the rescue.

Helmut Müller GmbH v Bundesanstalt für Immobilienaufgaben
This case was specifically brought to determine whether the sale of a piece of land for development constitutes a public works contract – the very issue that raised alarm in the Roanne case above.

Part of the procurement regulations[24] defines a public contract as: *"a contract for pecuniary interest concluded in writing between one or more economic operators and one or more contracting authorities and having as their object the execution of works, the supply of products or the provision of services."*

The same part then goes on to define a public works contract as: *"having as their object either the execution, or both the design and execution, of works related to one of the activities within the meaning of Annex I of the Directive, or a work, or the realisation, by whatever means, of a work corresponding to the requirements specified by the contracting authority"* where a "work" means the outcome of building or civil engineering works taken as a whole which is sufficient of itself to fulfil an economic or technical function.

---

24. Directive 2004/18

These definitions, to me, are not crystal clear and it is of little surprise that confusion arose. The Helmut Muller case provided some clarification.

In October 2006 the German Authority announced its intention to sell off 24 hectares of land on which stood a barracks, soon to be vacated. The land was valued at about €2.33million.

Helmut Muller (Muller) offered €4million, provided urban planning permission would be granted. The German Authority would not guarantee that and sought offers elsewhere. Muller then offered €1million but were outbid by an offer from GSSI (a competing bidder) of €2.5million.

Prior to finalising the deal, plans of the proposals for the land were requested and the authority, without any hard commitment, proceeded to work with GSSI on an urban development plan and the deal was finally struck with the contract specifying no particular future use for the land.

Muller challenged the sale on the basis that it should have been undertaken via an EU procurement process but the court rejected this.

However, the Oberlandesgericht Düsseldorf (a higher authority) was not convinced because it could foresee that construction work would – even if at some point in the future – constitute part of the deal. For assistance in its decision-making it referred some specific questions to the ECJ, seeking clarification of the definitions in Article 18 quoted above. (See? Even *they* weren't sure what the definitions meant – or were meant to mean).

The Oberlandesgericht Düsseldorf raised five specific points regarding the definition of a 'public works contract' – the nub of the issue – and I shall summarise them here, along with the ECJ's views in response.

1) Do the works (that arise) have to be carried out *for* the selling authority for its immediate economic benefit or is it sufficient for the works simply to be carried out in the public interest or for public benefit?

> With regards to the sale of land, the ECJ pointed out that to procure works, the authority would have to be a purchaser of services; selling land which was already built upon made the authority a seller and a construction project was not the purpose of the exercise. It was therefore deemed that the sale of the land to GSSI did not constitute a public works contract.
>
> Looking at the relationship between the authority and GSSI, the ECJ stated that there has to be an effective contract struck that secures for the authority direct service benefits for which a consideration was paid. The service in this case would have been the works and the authority would have had to have benefited 'directly.' In this context, 'directly' means:
>
> > a. The authority becomes the owner of the works or asset arising from the works or
> > b. The authority holds a legal right over the asset, which would be for the use or benefit of the public or
> > c. The authority will gain some economic advantage from the future use or sale of the asset (see the *Roanne* case, above).
>
> It was thus clarified that a 'public works contract' is one that 'directly benefits' the contracting authority, with the proviso that the works need not necessarily be *carried out* directly for the contracting authority.
>
> However, the Authority's control over the form of any subsequent development does not necessarily constitute

an interest, and their influence over development for the communal good is part of their duty as a social authority and does not constitute a direct beneficial interest (my words).

2) Does the contractor have to be under an obligation to carry out the works directly or can the contract be realised indirectly?

As you might expect, the fact that the contractor does the work directly or sub-contracts it is irrelevant so far as the obligation to do the works is concerned (this is true in all contracts). In a contract, the contractor has to see that the works are done and this requirement must be enforceable in law (i.e. it is a contract). A public works contract is no different.

3) Does the exercise of planning powers amount to a specification of works by the authority?

This refers directly to the definition in Article 18 (see above). Whilst the authority in the Muller case had stated it wanted to see proposals, it had not defined or otherwise influenced any of the design work. It had exercised its powers as an authority in matters of planning but this was not, the ECJ concluded, the same thing.

4) Is it possible for there to be a public concession when the economic operator (i.e. the contractor) already owns the land?

The answer is a straight 'no' because a concession applies when the contracting authority is in a position to carry out the service itself and they could not carry out the development on a piece of land they do not own. To us, now, this is obvious.

A point on this: concessions are outside of the EU Procurement Regulations and a concession has the characteristic that the concessionaire carries most of the operating risk. It was proposed in the challenge that GSSI carried a risk insofar as they could not be certain that planning permission would be granted for their proposals, if at all. The ECJ maintained that the risk was relevant to the statutory powers of the authority, and was not linked to the contract (of sale).

5) Should a sale of land and a subsequent development project be regarded as separate procurements?

The ECJ held that if the sale of land was intentionally part of a proposal to develop, the two could be perceived as one exercise, albeit made up of two phases, so the definition of a public works contract in Article 18 could apply to two-stage award procedures when the second stage will comprise a works contract.

In the case of Muller, there was no contractual binding on GSSI to build as part of the conditions of sale and there was no evidence that the authority had intended to progress along that route.

The outcome of all this was – in general terms:

a. Further clarification, following on from *Roanne*, separating an authority's obligations under planning law and their active influence in a development design or specification, which means the deal does not automatically come under the regime of the EU Procurement Regulations and
b. The separation of the land deal from the development stage, when strict criteria were applied to test the situation. The warning flag here is that the circumstances described above pertained specifically to the Muller case, and each case (i.e. from our point of view, each proposed land deal) must be seen and treated on its own merits.

Muller was one of those landmark cases that will be referred-to time and again. In fact, see the following example.

Midlands Co-Operative Society Ltd, R (on the application of) v Tesco Stores Ltd

On the face of it, a somewhat simpler case, this time regarding the sale of some land by Birmingham City Council (the Council) to Tesco Stores Ltd (Tesco), but often things don't turn out how you think they will...

In this instance, both Tesco and the Midland Co-Operative Society (Co-Op) obtained outline planning permission for the piece of land in question, on which was to be established a mixed-use development, probably anchored by a supermarket. Existing community facilities on the site were to be replaced and the Council's interest in them transferred to the developer as part of the deal.

Having secured these permissions, the Council decided, in 2006, to set up a competitive process – i.e. tender the opportunity – between Tesco and the Co-Op. The documentation stated that the Council wanted a development partner and laid down conditions regarding the timescales for the development to proceed. The replacement and transfer of the community facilities would be subject to negotiations.

Tesco and the Co-Op submitted bids and Tesco were the successful bidder; negotiations on issues such as the community facilities began and continued for over a year. Here's the first twist: Tesco then raised objections on the grounds that:

i.   negotiations took so long that the market on which they had based their bid had changed and

ii.   the stringent development requirements being laid down meant that it was not a land deal but a works contract and would have to be openly tendered in line with the EU Regulations.

In January 2010 (yes – four years after the first tender started) the Council decided to withdraw the tender and recommence another, new process.

This time the Council tendered for a 'land deal' which, with no specific development obligations, they considered would be EU exempt. Bidders had to submit development appraisals or proposals that would be assessed on the basis:

- Price – 70%
- Deliverability – 15%
- Conditionality – 15%

This time, the Co-Op raised an objection on the basis that the inclusion of a development appraisal meant that it was still subject to the EU Procurement Regulations and withdrew, deciding not to partake in a process that they considered sidestepped these legal requirements.

Tesco did submit a bid but the Council considered it non-compliant. Having got no bids, the Council decided to terminate this second process in August 2010.

Birmingham were not having a very good time but, full credit to them, they persevered.

The Council's third attempt went out as an open tender using an advert in the Estates Gazette, offering the site, occupied by the Community Facility, for sale. Tesco and the Co-Op were each invited to bid but the Co-Op declined on the basis that the deal was a 'sham' because the purpose behind the land sale was one of development and part of a wider regeneration objective.

Although 22 sets of tender documents had been issued, only Tesco submitted a bid and, surprisingly, won! Contracts were exchanged in early April 2011 and negotiations took place on the complex details of the deal which, out of interest, did not include the requirement to replace the Community Facility!

The Co-Op's turn again: they raised a challenge against the Council's award decision on three counts (including an issue around obligations under the 1972 Local Government Act and unfairness in the process) but relevant to our considerations here was their first ground of contravening the 2006 EU Procurement Regulations.

The Co-Op's claim in this respect was that the 'land deal' (my apostrophes) was inextricably linked to a requirement to develop, and hence it was part of a contract for construction – Land Deals are exempt from the EU Regulations but public construction contracts are not.

In considering judgement, the court referred to an earlier case (*Helmut Müller* – see above) where a public works contract was defined as one where there is a legally enforceable commitment on the contractor to perform relevant works. If any such requirement leaves an element of choice with the contractor as to whether they perform the work or not, then it is not a public works contract and in our instance here with Tesco it would be classed as a land deal.

Going further, the court stated that it is also necessary to look at the whole of the arrangement emanating from the deal and whether, through any, say, multi-stage process, there was at a later stage to be a commitment enforced upon the contractor to develop: simply distancing any such commitment from the land deal in this way would not suffice to exempt it from the regulations. However, if the authority merely intends to, or at most is very likely to, enter into a works contract at some time, this can be sufficiently far from a requirement or commitment to allow exemption from the 2006 Procurement Regulations. Not very clear or specific, I know, but that's what they said.

In the case of Tesco and the Co-Op, the commitment to develop was considered sufficiently remote from the agreement for it to not impact on the legality of the procurement as a land deal. This view was taken even in the light of the Council's original intention to develop on this site and on its plans to regenerate in a wider context. It's not the view I would have taken, but that final court decision held.

AG Quidnet Hounslow LLP v London Borough of Hounslow
Hounslow Council (Hounslow) wanted to develop a piece of land that lay next to one of two shopping centres and which was owned by Legal & General Assurance Society Ltd (L&G). Hounslow entered into discussions with L&G regarding the future of the site and at the same time were approached by AG Quidnet Hounslow LLP (Quidnet) on the same matter.

Hounslow entered into an agreement with L&G that each party would exercise best endeavours[25] to agree terms between them to develop the site and that in the meantime no other offers would be considered.

Quidnet brought a challenge through the High Court on the basis that:

- The proposed deal would be a public works contract and so should be tendered on the open market, and...
- If it were not a public works contract, the deal would still represent a breach of the EU Treaty, which requires freedom to provide services within and across the EU.

The challenge was interesting as it claimed a breach whichever way the court read the agreement. The court noted this, and decided to consider whether, if the EU Procurement Regulations did not apply, the requirements of the EU Treaty did.

You will recall that the EU Treaty (TFEU – Treaty on the Function of the European Union) requires that, even where a contract may not be subject to the EU Procurement Regulations, it must still be tendered in a manner that is at once fair and transparent and non-discriminatory[26]. Quidnet reckoned that the deal between Hounslow and L&G contravened this requirement.

---

25. See Chapter 16 – Good Faith and Reasonable Endeavours
26. Non-discriminatory: including and particularly with respect to cross-border trading opportunities

In making its decision, the court looked to (amongst others) the case of *Midlands Co-Operative Society Ltd, R (on the application of) v Tesco Stores Ltd* (see above) – a leading case on the matter of land deals and procurement – but noted that the Treaty (and Article 56 in particular) was broadly held to apply where the agreements concerned were analogous to contracts that come under the EU Procurement Regulations but are still exempt from them. An example would be Service Concessions[27] or perhaps works contracts below the EU threshold. In brief, whether a formal tender process is required or not, the opportunity must be advertised such that it is opened up to competition from the market.

The court's decision was based on a long and contorted process of logical argument that I shall not go into too deeply here. Although the Quidnet challenge was a bit of a first in cases of this nature, the court again resorted to considering whether there was any obligation on L&G to perform any services as part of the deal. It was concluded that L&G were under no obligation to perform any kind of service (such as a development) – it was merely an agreement to agree terms on a long lease of the land in question. In particular, there was no obligation on L&G to develop the land but any future works on the land would be provided for L&G as developers, not provided by them as contractors.

The Agreement was made the more remote from a development deal by the fact that any future management services provided by L&G would be for themselves and not for the benefit of the Council.

There were more considerations but the conclusion was that the Agreement made was purely for the interest in the land. On this basis, it was decided that the deal was solely a land deal, not a development deal, and so exempt from the EU Regulations.

Accepting this, then, did the deal transgress Article 56[28] *of the EU Treaty?*

27. Concessions do not have to follow the full EU procurement regime.
28. Article 56 deals with the right of a Member State to provide services to other Member States of the EU.

There were two (along with some other observations), relatively simple answers to that. Firstly, it was decided by the Court that the contract was not sufficiently akin to a contract that comes under the EU Regulations for Article 56 to have any effect. Secondly (and this surprises me) the Court noted that the deal was for a piece of land in England, between a UK Council and a UK company. Case Law is relatively light on the potential level of cross-border interest impacting on the relevance of Article 56 but the Court's conclusion was that international interest in such a local piece of land would have been low – the deal could 'safely' have been conducted as a matter internal to the UK.

Thus, Quidnet lost on that one, too.

Lessons from all of these: if you are involved in any procurement exercise that involves land, make sure you know – and then double check – whether it is EU exempt or not. The pickings from such deals can be rich and irritated third parties could challenge your process on the basis they were not invited to play.

What this means

> Land deals and development deals in general are complex and legal advice should be sought.

> If it is a pure land deal then the EU Regulations do not apply

> If it is a development deal, it is subject to the EU Regulations

> If it is a land deal that involves an element of construction, it is probably subject to the EU Regulations and the devil lies in the detail

> Much of the legal case history shows it is often hard to tell...

Cases:

- *Jean Auroux and Others v Commune de Roanne , Case C-220/05, judgment of 18 January 2007*
- *HelmutMüllerGmbHvBundesanstaltfürImmobilienaufgaben, Case-451/08 - judgment of 25 March 2010 .*
- *Midlands Co-Operative Society Ltd, R (on the application of) v Tesco Stores Ltd [2012] EWHC 620 (Admin)*
- *AG Quidnet Hounslow LLP v London Borough of Hounslow [2012] EWHC 2639 (TCC), judgment of 28 September 2012*

CHAPTER 11 – DISCLOSURE AT STANDSTILL

What is disclosure and what is Alcatel?
It often happens in law that when notable cases have an impact on practice the litigants attain fame through having their name bestowed upon the ensuing practice. 'Alcatel' is a standstill period that must be observed after a tender evaluation and before the award and signing of contracts and during which time the participants have a period of 'calm' to consider the outcome of the process, as advised in a Standstill or Alcatel Letter, ask for feedback on their submission and raise a challenge to the outcome if they so wish.

Regardless of any other timescales allowed within law for challenges to be levelled at a decision, the standstill period specifically facilitates the exchange of information (disclosure) so that a bidder may consider the outcome and highlight any anomaly or errors that they consider might have arisen in order that the matter may be resolved without recourse to the courts.

This doesn't often happen, it seems. Whilst it sounds simple enough, there are many cases in law that demonstrate it is not as easy as it sounds.

Alcatel Austria AG and Others v Bundesministerium für Wissenschaft und Verkehr
This is the case that started it all and the basis on which the standstill period (known as Alcatel) was introduced. Look out for long names...

The Bundesministerium für Wissenschaft und Verkehr (the Federal Ministry of Education and Research) issued a tender in May of 1996, using the open procedure, for the supply of various components for an IT system (you need know no more) for use on the Austrian Motorways. In September of that same year, the tenders having been evaluated, the outcome was decided and the contract signed on the same day to a company called Kapsch.

The other bidders (Alcatel) only learned of this through the press (!) and applied to have the decision set aside as there had been no time to consider the outcome. The fact was the Bundesvergabeamt (as it is called) had no powers to do this, regardless of the circumstances, as the contract had been signed, done and dusted.

A complaint was therefore lodged with the Constitutional Court – the *Verfassungsgerichtshof.* Oddly (to me) the *Bundesvergabeamt* had decided that some breaches had occurred but, as they could not do anything, brought the legal process to an end. However, following the complaint, the Constitutional Court set aside this decision.

The *Bundesvergabeamt* re-opened the case and, noting various breaches, set aside the award – technically, prohibited further performance of the contract - pending further consideration of the case, although *that* was held in abeyance following a counter-complaint by Austria!

At the time, the law in Austria did not require the Contracting Authority to make known the outcome of a bidding process to anyone save the successful tenderer and the acceptance of a bid was adequate to form the contract, even though the paperwork still had to be done (offer and acceptance – two key elements of a contract). The current legal standing could not overturn an outcome, merely award damages if errors in process had led to a mis-award.

Some complex and lengthy arguments ensued centring around how the law stood and the fact that, if interpreting the law so that the decision could be made known before the acceptance stage, any anomalies in the tendering process could be addressed before it was too late to sort things out – in other words, distinguishing between the decision regarding awarding the contract and actually concluding the contract and so incorporating a review period as referred to in Article 1 of the Directive 89/665 of the Council of the European Communities[29]. It is definitely written there, but no timescale is specified. In fact, Article 2 is quite strong on this matter, as well.

The argument then proceeded to ask what happens if these requirements have not passed into National law? Good point. This question was exacerbated by Austrian law (a) not requiring any public notification of a decision to award (or to intend to award) and (b) not having any period between the decision to award and the award itself.

The conclusion was that Member States have, in response to applications, the power to (and in fact *must*) review procurements in line with the provisions of the Directive and this whether there has been an award decision or not.

The case, the discussions and the final judgement, merely served to point out that something needed to be done to clarify the situation because it was recognised, amongst other things, that this process did not always allow a fair appraisal of the legitimacy of the process.

The European Ombudsman stepped in and after about a year a process was agreed that was officially called the Standstill Period but is called by everyone the Alcatel Period. The requirement was for a minimum 10 day pause after bidders (and other 'interested parties'[30]) had been notified of the outcome and this was further amended – and tightened up - by the Remedies Directive in 2009 (see Chapter 30).

Another case.

The Remedies Directive is quite specific on what information needs to be disclosed at the Alcatel stage but there is then the matter of what can the bidders ask to see as part of the debrief and their

29. Found at: http://eur-lex.europa.eu/LexUriServ/LexUriServ.do?uri=OJ:L:1989:395:00
33:0035:EN:PDF
30. This would include unsuccessful PQQ Applicants, if they have not already been
advised of the outcome of their Application.

endeavours to ensure that a fair process has been undergone? This was the nub of the case with *Croft House Care & Others v Durham CC.*

Croft House Care & Others (Croft) v Durham CC (Durham).
Durham had tendered for domestic care services and made the results known in February 2009. There was a challenge by one of the bidders (the reason not relevant to this matter), after which Durham changed the basis on which the bids were to be evaluated and re-ran the interviews (you may wish to have a look at Chapter 9 on criteria...).

In July 2009, when the final results were made known, three of the bidders who in February had been advised they had been awarded work (including Croft) found they were either being awarded less work than they had been told or none at all. The three issued proceedings claiming a breach of the EU Regulations, seeking a suspension of the tender process (i.e. halting it at the Alcatel stage) and seeking a set-aside of the award decision.

The issue that arose was an interesting and a practical one. The Council, at the first case management conference, wanted to keep certain documents confidential on the grounds that their disclosure would compromise the process if the court required the procurement to be re-run. In particular, the Council identified model answers and notes on the interview process which, if disclosed, would give the challenging bidders an advantage over other bidders if the process had to be re-run and so possibly make any distinction between future bidders virtually impossible.
Additionally, Durham claimed the disclosure would compromise the confidentiality of the other bidders in the event of a retendering process. I think these points sound reasonable.

The court, pragmatically, decided that the documents should be disclosed to the claimants' lawyers pending, and to enable, any further decision on confidentiality.

Durham classified documents in two ways:

- First, tenderers' submissions: the Council recognised that much of this might be disclosed because the tender documents had advised bidders that documentation may be subject to a Freedom of Information request and that anything considered commercially confidential should be marked as such (this matter should be covered in a standard paragraph in any ITT).
- Second, the Council's own documents: this was a more sensitive matter because, if the contents (the notes, etc. described above) were revealed, it would be almost impossible to re-run the procurement in a different way and still achieve the desired outcome.

The claimants disputed all Durham's claims for confidentiality on the basis of their not being allowed in law (they cited the Civil Procedure Rules) and not practical for them either as, being small firms, they had access to only limited outside advice.

Regarding bidders' submissions, the Court recognised there might be a need for confidentiality but also had to consider how much disclosure might be required to deal fairly with the claims. They also noted that no bidders had marked anything as commercially sensitive, but 12 bidders had raised such issues when they were advised of the possibility of disclosure.

The court decided that disclosure was relevant to the claimants' case and that disclosure should take place but, in recognition of the bidders' requests for confidentiality, instructed that there had to be redaction of certain key elements to maintain anonymity and remove unnecessary information.

The court also pointed out that the EU Procurement Rules do not override the Civil Procedure Rules, which is a point worth remembering.

Regarding Durham's own documentation, the Court noted two factors:

- firstly, the claimants were small businesses whose directors prepared the bids and attended the interviews and who could not afford a raft of legal advisers to take on the task of reviewing the tender documents and
- secondly that there may be some practical difficulties in re-running the tendering process if the degree of disclosure requested was granted.

On the first point, the court decided that the claimants could not properly instruct their lawyers if they did not have access to view the required documents – the whole point of reviewing a tender process, after all. The court therefore decided that the claimants could see the required documentation but with the proviso that the court would specify which documents could be seen. These included the bidders' PQQ and ITT submissions, evaluators' handwritten notes and Durham's guidance notes to the evaluation panel. However, all of the documents had to have names of evaluators and bidders redacted, notes on the contents could only be made that were passed to solicitors and no documents could be taken away from the viewing room (a solicitor's office).

On the second point, the court ruled that problems possibly encountered in a retender process could not be grounds for inhibiting (my phraseology) the due process of review. They acknowledged it may be *harder*, but not impossible. In fact, they argued that a greater understanding of Durham's requirements may actually improve the tender process! Regarding the risk of not being able to distinguish between bids the second time around, the court said that bidders would have to relate their own actual position, and not simply provide answers based on what the additional knowledge showed Durham was looking for – and a good tender process should be able to pick up on this. Whilst acknowledging it would be more difficult, the court said a re-tender was not made impracticable: just harder.

The main thing to draw from this is that even the evaluators' handwritten notes can be called upon in the event of challenge, and so it is essential the panel is made aware of this. Notes should be clear and factual and, of course, concentrate more on why a firm is marked down than why they have scored well – that is what bidders will be most interested in.

I also repeat – state how you are going to evaluate tender returns and do it – do not change part way through. In most cases, if a tender does go pear-shaped, a new tender starting from scratch is probably the best option. Sometimes it is the only option.

One more.

Roche Diagnostics Ltd v The Mid Yorkshire Hospitals NHS Trust
The Mid Yorkshire Hospitals NHS Trust (Yorkshire) tendered for laboratory services as a Managed Services Contract (an MSC). The ITT was issued on 23rd April 2012 and Roche Diagnostics Ltd (Roche) submitted a bid. On 2nd November, Roche was informed they had been unsuccessful, the award decision being in favour of Abbott Diagnostics Ltd (Abbott).

Roche challenged the decision on the basis that errors had been made in the financial assessments, leading to breaches of the 2006 Regulations. Roche were, however, unable to obtain documents that were a valid part of the actual evaluation process ("contemporaneous to it") and so applied to the Court for specific disclosure.

Yorkshire agreed to disclosure to a confidentiality ring: a limited group of essential persons sworn to confidentiality – principally the lawyers. However, what was disclosed was a spreadsheet that:

a. Had already been disclosed – with errors – but
b. Had subsequently been corrected and
c. Had been drawn up since the evaluation and so
d. Was not contemporaneous to it.

The spreadsheet did not really tick all the boxes.

Roche therefore continued to seek specific early disclosure of original documentation relating to the evaluation process. But they went further, because it transpired that Abbott had already been awarded an interim contract that included some of the work included in the contract for which Roche had tendered, so Roche sought early disclosure of the documents relating to that contract, too, because they considered the two matters were related and that the award of the interim contract also represented a breach of the 2006 Regulations.

The Court therefore had two issues to consider but, before we look at their view, a brief note or two on early disclosure.

Early Disclosure
Early disclosure is a process aimed essentially at trying to oil the wheels of law or even avoid litigation altogether by helping to clarify whether a court action is justified and hopefully saving money whether litigation goes ahead or not. However, such early disclosure can only be exercised when, in the event of litigation, such disclosure is fair to both parties and on the basis that discretion is exercised in the matter of detail.

In the case of Roche, the Court considered the circumstances and laid down the principles that should apply to early disclosure, namely:

a. The challenger should be promptly provided with the documentation that relates to the actual evaluation to enable an informed view to be formed of the process, all provided the bounds of confidentiality and proportionality are observed[31]
b. The short time limits the Regulations allow for action to be taken confirms this as an appropriate procedure to follow[32]

31. Confidentiality – care not to reveal anything that might breach commercial confidentiality or impede any repeat procurement exercise. Proportionality – disclosure of documents that actually relate to the issue, with no undue demands.
32. Remember – the time is calculated from the time when the challenger knew, or *should* have known, of the infringement.

c. Each application for early disclosure must be considered on its individual merits, drawing a distinction between instances where the claimant has good grounds for raising a challenge as opposed to a disgruntled bidder who is merely upset at not winning

d. The scope of the early disclosure must be tightly drawn and focus on documentation at the core of the dispute – for example the actual evaluation documentation, as completed at the time

e. The Court must balance a genuine need for information on the part of the claimant and what may be a simple 'fishing' exercise, trying to shore up an otherwise weak claim, leading to the defendant encountering unnecessary and so unfair costs.

Back to Roche.

On the matter of the tender evaluation, the Court considered early disclosure would be appropriate and perhaps even allow the matter to be settled without further litigation (so saving costs); Yorkshire had maintained that the matter related to the ITT documentation so the requested evaluation paperwork was not relevant but the Court stated clearly that the very fact that Yorkshire had so far failed to provide consistent responses to the request for information on the evaluation process had merely served to fuel the challenger's suspicions of ineptness. The Court further stated that, even if Yorkshire is correct, Roche were entitled to draw their own conclusion.

The Court, however, only allowed disclosure of some of the requested documentation, stating that it considered some were not essential to Roche's understanding of the case and these could be revealed as part of standard Disclosure later in the event of a case being pursued. So Roche won that bit but they did not get all that they asked for.

Regarding the interim contract, the Court needed to know:

- why a contract had been let that Roche may have been eligible to tender for
- why it was for works covered by the MSC for which Roche did tender and
- why, if the works were essential for patient care whilst the legal delays to the contract were resolved, the existing contract was terminated seemingly too early. Also,
- how come Abbott was awarded the MSC shortly after it had been awarded (seemingly in secret) the interim contract? Was that just a coincidence?

A lot of questions...

The Court therefore decided to allow early disclosure of documents relating to the letting of the interim contract and the work it covered because it would be unfair to expect Roche to commence proceedings with so little information at their disposal. The Court required disclosure of:

- Documents relating to Yorkshire's process for seeking quotes for the interim contract, why and when Abbott were approached and why Roche were not
- The interim contract itself
- What works were included and which of these overlapped the contract for which Roche had tendered.

This seems a fairly extensive list, and it is, but in keeping with the 5 principles laid out above, the list of documents requested by Roche which were *not* approved by the Court was even longer and included details of why Yorkshire felt it necessary to let the interim contract at all, whether Abbott was already an incumbent at the laboratory and in any current or intended future contracts at other laboratory sites.

This was a fairly complex case in some ways, and it all relates to disclosure – the outcome of the actual challenge (at time of going to press) has yet to be seen. It does, though, give a clear steer on the machinations involved in deciding what paperwork can be asked for in the event of a challenge, and which of that can be secured by law before the case even actually goes to court.

Lesson – make sure all evaluation paperwork is complete, clear, factual and relevant and avoid any ambiguous or inappropriate notes or comments, even in personal 'notes to self' on the part of any evaluators.

What this means

> A standstill period lasting a minimum of 10 days is required after the evaluation is complete and before any award is actually made; this period is kicked off by the issuing of the Alcatel letter

> The letter or notice (Alcatel or standstill latter) is sent to each bidder advising them of the outcome of the tender process and their performance compared with the winning bid (quite specific stuff is required so, if you are not sure, seek further advice on this)

> Requests for further feedback are common during this period – they are not challenges

> In the letter, you can only reveal details of that bidder's score and the name and score of the winning bid. Background information and details of other participants is not to be disclosed.

> Disclosure of this additional information has to be secured through the courts, when it is usually a precursor to or part of a formal challenge

> The court may or may not allow disclosure or early disclosure (designed to avoid expensive court action), depending on the circumstances

> Disclosure may be to a Confidentiality Ring – a group normally

consisting of lawyers who view and report on the documentation so far as the case requires, but which keeps the remainder of the information confidential

> Requests for disclosure via the courts can be a complex legal battle in their own right

---

Cases:

- *Alcatel Austria AG and Others, Siemens AG Österreich and Sag-Schrack Anlagentechnik AG v Bundesministerium für Wissenschaft und Verkehr (Case C-81/98)*
- *Croft House Care Ltd & Ors v Durham County Council ([2010] EWHC 909 (TCC)), 27 April 2010*
- *Roche Diagnostics Ltd v The Mid Yorkshire Hospitals NHS Trust [2013] EWHC 933 (TCC).*

CHAPTER 12 – DISCRIMINATION

Not just your everyday sort of discrimination.
Discrimination in procurement law is the same as in any other sort of law except that it tends to crop up when terms or requirements restrict firms from working across borders rather than the more common forms that hit the papers on a daily basis.

Very often, such discriminatory requirements appear as tendering criteria and your attention is drawn to Chapter 9 that deals in some detail with criteria.

You will (or ought to) know that the EU Treaty stipulates non-discrimination as one of its key requirements in all tender processes, even those that are below the EU thresholds, because it recognises the natural desire to encourage and support businesses in the host country; the EU logic is that *all* firms can work abroad across borders in the EU, so the playing field is already balanced and does not need tilting.

The *Erga Ose* case is a good illustration.

Commission v Hellenic Republic
Erga Ose AE was a Greek railway transport company who, in October 2003, published an OJEU Notice for an Open tender for various engineering and design services. The Notice laid down the key criteria for eligibility, which included the requirement that firms had to be Greek companies enrolled on the corresponding national register and had to possess a certificate or, if not Greek, must possess formal and substantive qualifications equivalent to those required for Greek consultants who are enrolled on the Greek register of consultants. Further, foreign consultants must have staff for each discipline corresponding to the staff required for Greek consultancy firms. This was quite stringent, but on the face of it reasonable, but it then went on to say: *"it is stressed that foreign consultancy firms/consultants who submitted an expression of interest in an ERGA OSE AE tendering procedure*

in the six months preceding the date of their expression of interest in the present competition and who declared qualifications corresponding to certificate categories different from those now being asked for will not be accepted".

This is a mouthful – you may need to read it twice - and, in the end, the Court agreed that the wording was discriminatory, but not in the way you (or I) would have expected. The Notice did not forbid foreign equivalent qualifications (which is normal) provided they had staff qualified in a way equivalent to that required to meet the Greek certification requirements.

The ECJ did not rule that the 'offending' clause was illegal in itself but it did decide that the nature of the wording was such that foreign practices would be deterred from entering a bid and that this in itself was sufficient for it to be considered discriminatory.

What this means

> Do not try and favour or disfavour any particular provider or nationality or sector or 'type' in your tender documentation – and do not give the *impression* that you have. If the impression is there, that is sufficient to uphold a challenge. So...

> Be careful what your words convey: is it what you actually meant them to say? This problem has cropped up elsewhere in this book and emphasises the benefits of having someone else read your words (even better if the reader knows nothing about the topic on which you are writing)

> Have a person's views not only on 'does this make sense' and 'any typos?' but also 'in your view, what does this actually *mean*?'

> Try and cut down wordiness in documents such as a PQQ or a tender, but do *not* do so at the expense of absolute clarity – it will always come back to bite you at some time or another

Cases

- *Commission v Hellenic Republic, judgment of 12 November 2009 Case C-199/07*

CHAPTER 13 – ELIGIBILITY TO TENDER

What does 'eligibility' mean?
Eligibility to Tender in this context covers issues around a party being entitled to tender by virtue of, say, their status or nature rather than their failure as a body to meet the requirements of evaluation criteria.

As a general example, an organisation that has contravened any of the crimes listed in Regulation 23 of the Public Contracts Regulations 2006 may be able to pass all the assessment criteria and, in fact, may be able to perform the contract admirably, but that is not even relevant. It is not legal, under Regulation 23, for a contracting authority to knowingly consider an organisation eligible to bid if that organisation or any of its *"...directors or any other person who has powers of representation, decision or control of the economic operator..."* have committed any of the offences that the Regulation lists – in some detail. These offences include criminal conspiracy, corruption, bribery, fraud, cheating the Revenue, etc., etc. Regulation 23 is quite long.

It is therefore prudent to issue with any initial tender documents (for example, with the Pre-Qualification Questionnaire package) a statement, quoting Regulation 23, with guidance explaining that firms who are ineligible under Regulation 23 cannot partake in the process, and asking them to confirm that neither the Applicant firm as a body nor any of its decision-makers have committed any of the offences listed in it.

That is the big story. However, the question of eligibility crops up in case law as well, where criteria for eligibility (again, not *evaluation* criteria) laid down by the contracting authority come into question.

European Ombudsman inquiry into complaint 491/2007/PB against the European Commission
This case is interesting on two counts:

1) It is not about contravening the 2006 Procurement Regulations
2) It was the European Commission itself (the EC) that faced the challenge.

The complaint concerned an advertisement for a tender to provide information services for the EC itself, at its public information desk in Berlin. An unsuccessful bidder challenged the process via the Ombudsman on the ground, amongst others, that eligibility criteria were such that they contravened certain rules relating to fairness and non-discrimination.

Whilst the EC does not, itself, have to comply with EU Procurement Law as such (interpreted as our Procurement Regulations of 2006), it does have to comply with financial regulations that govern the spending of all European budget money. I will not bore you with a list of all the regulations and directives that apply but will confirm that these regulations require that any procurement covered by the regulations must comply with the known (by us) principles of proportionality, equal treatment and non-discrimination.

The complainant advocated that the stated requirement that all bidders had to have operational staff that were qualified to degree level in political science, specialising in European law, or the equivalent contravened these treaty principles. The complainant alleged that the post was a Grade C level appointment – equivalent to a secretary and normally requiring a basic education - and that the tasks could be performed equally well by persons having qualifications other than political science at that level of specialisation.

The complainant also stated that the selection criteria did not reflect the tasks as detailed in the tender documents – but we are not here to look at criteria, so shall leave that one alone.

The EC responded that the post was in the centre of the Governmental area of Berlin and had to provide high-level information to a range of persons, including government officials.

The Ombudsman found that the tender was advertised as providing advice and information to the general public; it was not aimed at government officials and so he could not agree that the requirement for a degree in political science specialising in European law was justified. He felt that the eligibility criterion unnecessarily restricted competition and found in favour of the complainant.

My personal view is that it might also have contravened the requirement for proportionality but that issue did not arise. Even so, the message is to make sure that, when you set the bar for Applicants or bidders, it is set at a height that is appropriate for the task being tendered.

Assitur Srl v Camera di Commercio, Industria, Artigianato e Agricoltura di Milano

I advised early on in the book that there might be overlaps, and this is one. Whilst this case is being considered in a chapter on eligibility to bid, the cause for the discussion is the possibility of, or the possible *accusation* of, collusion between bidders, so it could easily have been placed in Chapter 6. But it wasn't – eligibility rather than collusion is more the key point in this case so I have put it here.

The contract, tendered by Milan Chamber of Commerce (Milan) in 2003, was for courier services. Three firms were in the running and one of them – Assitur – claimed that the other two - SDA Express Courier Spa (SDA) and Poste Italiane Spa – were linked.

The risk of and potential for collusion if 'linked' companies are tendering are obvious but is it automatically right or fair to exclude either or both from the process? My personal view, prior to this case, was that one or the other ought to withdraw (depending, of course, on the closeness of the relationship, although this would itself be open to debate) but I have had to revise that view.

As you know, the EU Regulations are interpreted into national law and the Italian law had clauses preventing bids from firms that were linked by degrees of control to other firms bidding. In this case, SDA's ultimate controller was Poste Italiane. Milan considered and rejected the claim on the basis that the Italian Regulations did not prohibit the two companies from bidding and awarded the contract to SDA.

Assitur challenged through the Italian courts, who referred the matter to the ECJ.

Article 29 of Directive 92/40 lays down seven criteria that preclude economic operators from bidding. The thrust of the query to the ECJ, in an effort to resolve the challenge, was 'is this list exhaustive?' Whilst the intention was that it should be, there is nothing to prevent member countries laying down additional rules if they are aimed at ensuring equal treatment and transparency. However, any such additional rules must observe the principles of proportionality and not be such that, by preventing firms from bidding, they restrict open competition.

To this end, it was also necessary that any rules recognise that associated firms can and in fact do operate independently and that they could submit bids without collusion or influence and not distort the competition. The conclusion was, therefore, that any rules should not be such that associated firms could not demonstrate their bids were not, or would not be, influenced by any associated bidding firms.

Of course, the risk of collusion is there, and firms need to be able to demonstrate their independence within the tender process and any suspicion of such collusion would have to be carefully investigated. If such influence were found, the participants would have to be excluded from the proceedings (that is obvious) but the key is that neither a mere commercial relationship nor a degree of financial or other control is sufficient to exclude a company from a procurement exercise.

Thus, any national law that blanket-prohibits associated or related firms from bidding cannot be upheld. The challenge was not successful in that accepting bids from the associated companies was not unlawful.

Conclusion: bids from related companies can cause concern but outright prohibition of any bid on that basis alone is unlawful. Firms must have the chance to demonstrate that they will not (or cannot) collude. You thus have the right to ask for this assurance: it may be their independent structure, the creation of 'Chinese walls' or a simple, written undertaking, but you cannot easily exclude any party other than on the basis of proof of collusion in the preparation of the bid. Such proof – which may have to stand up in court – may be hard to establish.

What this means

> Eligibility to tender can crop up as an issue on several counts, in addition to performance against evaluation criteria

> Regulation 23 forbids an organisation from tendering – and you from inviting them to bid – if they have committed any of a whole list of misdemeanours (see Chapter 29). Get bidders to confirm that they haven't, at an early stage in the process

> Potential bidders can be barred from tendering by not meeting stringent minimum requirements such as an accreditation or a qualification. Take care not to require as a minimum something you do not need or is, in fact, not essential – an issue which also has a smack of proportionality about it

> Closely-associated firms *may* not both be eligible to bid for the same contract: it has to be demonstrated that they cannot (or will not) collude with each other and so distort the tender process. Bear in mind that two such companies may not *automatically* be barred from bidding

Cases:

- *European Ombudsman inquiry into complaint 491/2007/PB against the European Commission (Jan 2002)*
- *Assitur Srl v Camera di Commercio, Industria, Artigianato e Agricoltura di Milano, judgment of 19 May 2009e C538/07*

CHAPTER 14 – ERRORS (IN SUBMISSIONS)

How forgivable is it to make a mistake?
It is not unusual for a company to contact you and say that they have made an error in their submission and to ask if they can correct it. We probably think we know what the answer should be but shall look at a couple of cases so that, even if we were right all along, we will at least be able to quote some case law to support our response.

Harrow Solicitors and Advocates R (on the application of) v The Legal Services Commission
The Legal Services Commission (LSC) issued a tender for the provision of publicly-funded immigration work.

Tendering for legal services, like IT and financial services (and some other things, probably), is not always as straightforward as other procurement categories, so bear with me. The contract would be awarded for three years for a certain number of 'matter starts' (cases). To be eligible, bidders had to meet certain essential criteria. If the capacity of the bidders (combined) exceeded the number of 'matter starts' required, additional 'selection criteria' would be invoked to reduce the number of eligible bidders. The level of response meant this additional stage had to be used.

One particular scoring point was the provision of an advertised drop-in facility, available at least once a week, and this would be worth two points.

The scoring mechanism was such that a score of 34 to 38 points would give bidders their full quota of requested 'matter starts' and those who scored 33 would get a proportion of the 'matter starts' that remained. Not too simple, but it has a logic.

Harrow Solicitors and Advocates (Harrow) scored 31 points – two short of the minimum – but realised on feedback that they had inadvertently entered 'No' to the question on drop-in services when in fact they already actively provided two such sessions per week. It was a genuine error.

Harrow immediately appealed to LSC but LSC declined to reconsider as it felt it had a duty to be fair and equal to all parties: it was Harrow's job to ensure the bid was accurate before submitting it and they could not allow Harrow to amend its bid after submission.

Harrow went to judicial review of this decision.

The High court found in favour of LSC, which I suppose is fairly obvious in some respects, but some of the observations made in reaching that decision are interesting:

- The principles of equal treatment and good administration would be violated if a bidder were allowed to amend a bid after the tender deadline[33]
- This does not mean that clarifications cannot be sought (albeit 'properly')
- Clarifications are sought in instances of ambiguity – yes / no answers generally require no clarification
- If no ambiguity is seen, then no clarification will be sought – the onus is on the bidder to get it right
- In particular, changing 'No' to 'Yes' would go beyond clarification – it would constitute changing the bid
- In the case of Harrow, the court said that, despite the fact that the error was easily verifiable (because they were already delivering a drop-in service), the onus was not on the Contracting Authority to determine this and besides...
- The tender asked about providing a drop-in service for the proposed contract, not about current provisions (an interesting point – remember looking back (PQQ stage) and forwards (the tender stage)?)
- The tender was 'true' in that the answers were clear-cut: putting

---

33. Of course, an early submission can be withdrawn and replaced by an amended submission before the deadline.

'No' instead of 'Yes' could not be seen by the evaluators as an error and, put simply, if that is what you say, that is what you are submitting (my words), and this is supported by the fact that...

- The tender period was eight weeks – ample time for Harrow to have checked (and double-checked) their submission.
- Importantly – the mistake was Harrow's own – LSC had made no error in its process

Interestingly, the next example also involves the Legal Services Commission and an e-tendering process and again has several lessons embedded within it.

Hoole & Co v Legal Services Commission

Hoole & Co (Hoole) submitted a bid to provide legal services in the field of immigration and asylum in a tender process executed by the Legal Services Commission (LSC). The process was run using the LSC's internet-based e-tendering portal.

In this case, in simple terms, the bidder had to complete an on-line form, using a drop-down menu to select and save the required options. Once completed, Hoole printed one part of their submission but (they claimed) found the form was blank. A check of the on-line version confirmed to them that the selections had been made and saved so it was assumed that the anomaly was part of a confidentiality safeguard. They duly submitted their bid.

When the bids were opened, LSC informed Hoole that their bid had been rejected on the grounds that certain critical parts of their bid were blank.

Hoole applied for a judicial review on the following grounds:

- There must have been a failure on the part of LSC's software
- The technology supporting the tendering process was so inadequate as to confuse the bidder and mislead them into thinking that a bid had been successfully submitted
- The LSC had breached their duty of fairness in not informing

them that essential information was missing from their submission.

Technical expertise was drawn on to evaluate the tendering system used. They found that:

- If not used in the manner advised (i.e. responses to be entered in the correct order), some data would indeed not be saved but the instructions in this regard were clear and adequate.
- Whilst there had been some early issues regarding the compatibility of some systems with the LSC system, these had been addressed and adequate information given on overcoming these problems.
- There was no technical problem with the LSC system.
- (Surprisingly) it was not possible for a printout to show data different to that which had been saved on the system.

The High Court found as follows:

- Whilst Hoole honestly believed they had submitted a bid, they had not, in fact, done so.
- This failure to submit was not due to any fault on the part of the LSC or due to its tendering system
- Because of a complexity in the evaluation process, bidders were not required to complete all boxes or even bid for all parts of the package available; thus blank fields in a submission would not automatically give rise to concern.
- Whilst evidence showed that Hoole had misunderstood some other parts of the tendering instructions, there was no evidence to show that other bidders had trouble submitting their tenders.
- Having found a discrepancy between the screen version and the printout, Hoole should have made enquiry to the tendering system helpdesk.

Hoole wanted a Judicial Review so as to allow them to re-submit their bid with the missing information inserted. The High Court ruled against this on the following grounds:

- The system was not defective.
- Whilst major ambiguities in tendering instructions or other such problems (my words) may justify an opportunity for bidders to clarify their submissions where it is practical to do so, in this instance there was no such justification and so to afford Hoole the opportunity would, in fact, be considered unfair but in Hoole's favour, i.e. discriminating against the other bidders who would not have the opportunity to amend their submissions.
- Similarly, a bidder cannot be given an opportunity to make corrections or alterations to their submission if the errors are not due to a fault on the part of the contracting authority.
- In fact, declining the opportunity to amend the bid meant that the Contracting Authority had acted with fairness and equanimity.

These two examples both relate to e-tendering processes, and it is a fact that such issues tend to arise more with these because bidders often have problems through uploading tenders at busy times (i.e. submitting too late) or not fully understanding the process. Firms are generally much more practiced at hard-copy submissions (although this is changing), when there tends to be less room for pleas for clemency: what they wrote and when they delivered it are plain facts.

The message for e-tendering is writ large: make the tendering instructions overtly clear, advise against last-minute submissions and, provided your e-system is working well, stand firm when requests are made for leeway to submit late or amend a bid's content. Case Law is behind you.

The message concerning allowing amendments after the tender deadline generally is: don't. Omissions or errors in a submission are down to the bidder – what they submit is what they submit and the onus is on them entirely to make it right.
Exceptions or areas of greyness may crop up where there is a contradiction within the bid – for example, a tally of sub-totals does

not match the bottom line submission[34] - and there are processes for dealing with this (the documentation should advise what the process would be), but plain errors of statement or fact, as a rule, cannot be granted any leeway.

What this means

> Submission errors tend to be more common when using e-tendering systems so make sure the process is clearly defined and warn bidders to leave enough time before the deadline to upload the material – it can often take a long time

> The onus is on the bidder to ensure that all required documents are submitted by the stated time

> Unless submission problems are down to the client or their system, late submissions can rarely – if ever - be accepted

> Errors or omissions within the body of a submission are *wholly* the responsibility of the bidder and what is submitted has to be taken at face value, regardless of what else you may know

---

Cases:

- *Harrow Solicitors and Advocates R (on the application of) v The Legal Services Commission ([2011] EWHC 1087 (Admin)), judgment of 28 April 2011*
- *Hoole & Co (a firm), R (on the application of) v Legal Services Commission, [2011] EWHC 886 (Admin) judgment of 15 April 2011.*

---

34. As an example, see JCT procedures Alternative 1 and Alternative 2

CHAPTER 15 – EXPERT EVIDENCE

Not always as good as it seems...
Expert Evidence is that where the court needs to apprise itself of facts or knowledge outside of the court's own expertise. Up until recently, expert witnesses were immune from law suits for breach of duty, but now that has changed.

Jones v Kaney
Jones had been hit by a car and instructed Dr Kaney, as a clinical psychologist, to prepare a report to support his case for personal injuries against the driver. It was unfortunate that Dr Kaney (wrongly) signed a joint statement agreeing with the driver's insurer's expert that Jones had exaggerated his injuries, to the point where he had been deceptive and deceitful.

Jones, not surprisingly, sued Kaney for breach of duty and Kaney claimed exemption from suit on the back of two old cases[35]. Whilst this defence was originally upheld, the Jones case, by appeal, reached the Supreme Court and this court held that, in law, every wrong should have a means of redress and allowed the appeal.

The decision was not unanimous – it was a majority view of five to two. The counter-view was that, if expert witnesses were not immune from prosecution, they would be deterred from presenting at court. This was countered on the basis that experts persistently provide advice for which they may be sued and take insurance out to cover that eventuality. Being an expert witness did not preclude anyone from a duty of care and their obligations under the Supply of Goods and Services Act of 1982, which itself is supported by various case law.

If you are being called as an expert witness or if you are commissioning one, you would be well advised to bear this in mind.

The corollary of this is, if commissioning an expert witness, make sure you get a good one. A more recent case illustrates this further.

---

35. Dawkins v Rokeby in 1873 and Hargreaves v Bretherton in 1959

National Museums and Galleries on Merseyside (Trustees of) v
AEW Architects and Designers Ltd and another
This is one of those cases where the proceedings get a bit messy and
those being sued sue others down the line (i.e. pass the buck) and so
on. I shall try to avoid losing touch with the purpose of reciting the
case, concentrating primarily on the matter of the expert witness
called to give evidence in defence of the architects against whom
a suit of defective design had been lodged by the Trustees of the
National Museums and Galleries on Merseyside (the Museum).

The claim was for defects in design and construction and the
essence of the case was factual in terms of failings in the outcome
of the project (for which the architects in turn sued the builders
– Galliford Try). The faults themselves were not in question, but
the matter of liability was, and it is suspected that the insurers,
because of this, may have made the resolution more tortuous than
it might otherwise have been.

Anyway, the defendants (AEW) declined to give evidence
(considered odd at the time) and instead relied on an expert
witness. However, this expert witness declared under cross-
examination that he was "seeking to defend the indefensible for
the [defendants'] benefit", which is not what you want to hear from
your prime witness. The judge was similarly unimpressed and
stated categorically that he considered him "wholly unconvincing
about all aspects of liability" and summarily discounted all of his
evidence.

It transpired, extraordinarily, that the expert – new to giving such
evidence - had not been instructed to give due consideration to
what might have been expected of the defendants in their role as
architects.

The case was lost – no surprise there – and there was some
wrangling over liability between the two defendant parties inside
and out of the courts, but all in all the matter gave rise to damages
of over £1million. This is no small beer, so make sure your witness

is [a] an expert who is [b] experienced and is [c] able to advocate on your behalf. All obvious stuff, but not always realised.

One more, with a twist.

BY Development Ltd and others v Covent Garden Market Authority
BY Development Ltd (BY) were unsuccessful bidders in a tender for a development contract for New Covent Garden Market and brought a challenge against the award decision, claiming the Authority made 'manifest' errors in its assessment of the bids and that the BY bid was treated unfairly[36].

The accusation of 'manifest errors' was levelled at issues around planning and finance and BY requested admission of evidence by an expert witness. Covent Garden Market Authority (CG) contested this request, counter-claiming that it was neither admissible nor relevant.

A word here on the court's rôle in the instance of challenges regarding the 2006 Public Contract Regulations.

1. The courts can only form a view on whether there was a manifest error or an element of unfairness in the way a decision was reached: it cannot review the tender process *per sé*[37] or compare the merits of different bids.
2. In particular, a manifest error is one that is obvious and indisputable, which can be demonstrated as having disregard of the facts.

These two points lead to the conclusion that rarely, if ever, is there a need or justification for an expert witness in cases of this nature. In this instance, as would generally be the case, the evaluation panel would have comprised persons who would have either been experts in their fields themselves or would have been advised by

36. We will not look at this aspect of the challenge here.
37. You are referred to the Chapter 4, *Virgin challenges DfT,* – you cannot level a challenge under the EU Regulations on the grounds that a procurement has been done badly – only if it has been done *wrongly*.

those who were. This is not tantamount to a blanket ban – as we have seen above – but means there has to be specific justification for an expert witness to be accepted to provide evidence.

In the BY case we are looking at, the court decided that an expert witness was not justified and rejected the application. It conceded that if, after hearing both sides' evidence, some expert clarification *was* required, an expert would be mutually sought between the two parties to resolve the matter.

An aside to this is that, in effect, the expert witness would have been deciding on a matter of manifest error – which is, in fact, the rôle of the court, so the court could not allow that. Bit of a riddle, really.

This was a good outcome for contracting authorities in that their ability to withstand a challenge may be somewhat enhanced. The moral for us is do not simply accept at face value any threat that an expert witnesses will be called to support a challenge.

What this means

> You will not often encounter expert witnesses in cases around procurement process, but they may crop up and perhaps more so in cases around the conduct of a contract

> If you employ an expert witness make sure they understand the brief and are on your side

> Do not panic if the 'other side' employ an expert witness: you may need to employ your own expert to balance the weight of opinion or you may be able to have their request to use an expert witness declined by the court

> If *you* are asked to appear as an expert witness, remember that you will no longer be immune from claims if your client feels your evidence was not suitable or constructive to their case

Cases:

- *Jones v Kaney [2011] UKSC 13 (29 March 2011)*
- *National Museums and Galleries on Merseyside (Trustees of) v AEW Architects and Designers Ltd and another [2013] EWHC 2403 (TCC) (1 July 2013 and 20 August 2013)*
- *BY Development Ltd and others v Covent Garden Market Authority [2012] EWHC 2546 (TCC), judgment of 28 September 2012*

CHAPTER 16 – GOOD FAITH & REASONABLE ENDEAVOURS

A popular turn of phrase
I include this topic as the term 'reasonable endeavours' and similar are often used in contracts to ensure bidders do their best to achieve where we know there may be an element of doubt as to what is exactly possible.

As in some other chapters, I have included something which, in effect, relates primarily to contracts and contract terms (or the specification, of course) because, as I always advocate, you cannot separate the procurement from the contract – at all.

EDI Central Ltd v National Car Parks Ltd
National Car Parks Ltd (NCP) were the tenants of a car park and contracted developer EDI to develop the site, and the Agreement included a clause stating that both parties *"shall use all reasonable endeavours to achieve the main objectives [of the Agreement] and shall act in good faith..."*

The case was brought because NCP considered that EDI had not used 'all reasonable endeavours' in its pursuit of the objectives and EDI contested this, claiming that no developer would have pursued the project at that time due to a range of external reasons that meant the outcome would reap no commercial benefit.

The court agreed that, once it was realised that any obstacle could not be overcome then there was no merit in pursuing the objective any further.

Whilst this was a case in Scotland, there are issues here that pertain in all the UK. The judge observed that best endeavours may not require much more effort than all reasonable endeavours, since *"it is difficult to conceive that an obligation to use best endeavours requires a party to take steps which are unreasonable."* In other words, however you phrase it, the courts would not expect any party to take any unreasonable or commercially imprudent actions simply to comply with the contract.

On good faith clauses, the judge opined that good faith required the duty to:

- observe reasonable commercial standards of fair dealing
- have faithfulness to the agreed common purpose and
- exercise consistency with the expectations of the other party, requiring them to ...
- genuinely do their best to achieve the desired result and not merely to go through the motions

Such clauses are becoming increasingly popular in contracts and, as is shown, are less onerous than might be perceived. However, it may serve to avoid contention later on if you can establish what might be expected of either party under the term 'reasonable endeavours,' 'best endeavours' and 'good faith' and hopefully establish when a potential obstacle might be defined as insurmountable or how it might be agreed as such.

What this means

> Clauses requiring 'Good Faith', 'Best Endeavours', etc. are being used more often in contracts but in reality have little legal bite – the courts are looking more and more towards reasonableness in their judgements

> So using these clauses to ensure an outcome that suits you regardless of any obstacles will not wash

> If you choose to use such clauses, it is advisable to define them within the contract so that, in the event of a dispute, the expectations and subsequent legal commitment are clear

> Avoid using these phrases as a lazy substitute for more specific clauses

Cases:

* *Edi Central Ltd v National Car Parks Ltd [2010] ScotCS CSOH_141, 27 October 2010 .*

CHAPTER 17 – INEFFECTIVENESS

When things got scary...
One of the larger 'scares' of the procurement world was the introduction of the Remedies Directive in 2009, under which it became mandatory (yes – mandatory) for a court to cancel or render ineffective a contract where it had been awarded in the face of specific breaches of the EU Procurement Regulations. The Remedies Directive is dealt with specifically in a succeeding chapter so I will not dwell on it *per sé* here, but will look at one of the very first cases where the issue has arisen, by way of illustration.

The case is very complex, and has many strands, so I will be selective with what I cover and the amount of detail I give to save muddying the waters. Even so, it is not simple.

Alstom Transport v Eurostar International Ltd & Another
The contract was for the design, supply and maintenance of high speed trains for Eurostar and had been awarded to Siemens through the Negotiated Procedure, initiated by an ITN[38] issued in May 2009.

A year later (to the month) Eurostar informed Alstom that the contract was intended to be awarded to Siemens but that they would remain reserve bidder. On 18th August 2010, Eurostar entered into a preliminary Agreement with Siemens and on 5th October they informed Alstom that they had been unsuccessful and that the contract was to be awarded to Siemens, following a 10-day standstill period.

On the 19th October Alstom initiated High Court proceedings in an attempt to secure an injunction to prevent the award of the contract to Siemens.

On the 29th October the High Court refused Alstom's application despite recognising that their case had some serious issues to be

---

38. ITN – Invitation to Negotiate

tried in relation to breaches of the regulations. Nevertheless, the court considered, on 'balance of convenience', that it would be unjust and inappropriate to freeze the award.

Eurostar completed the contract with Siemens on 3rd December 2010 and informed Alstom accordingly.

On 4th May 2011, Alstom applied to have its claim amended to include new material and seek a declaration of ineffectiveness of the final contract between Eurostar and Siemens.

The defendants (Eurostar) claimed that the action was unjustified on the basis that:

a. The Regulations did not apply to the procurement
b. The grounds did not exist for the remedy of ineffectiveness to apply and
c. The action was, in any event, out of time.

The following points supported the validity of the Alstom action:

a. The Regulations do apply to the procurement and
b. The contract eventually entered into by Siemens and Eurostar was materially different to that being sought through the tender process (you are referred to Chapter 5 on contract changes).

The Remedies Directive lays down three grounds for ineffectiveness. In brief, the two relevant to this case are:

1. Where the contract has been awarded without prior publication of a notice in the Official Journal in any instance where the Regulations require such a notice.
2. Comprises four parts:
    a. the contract has been entered into in breach of any requirement imposed by the standstill period
    b. there has also been a breach of the utilities duties under the Regulations

   c. the breach in bullet (a) has deprived the economic operator of the possibility of starting proceedings in respect of the other breach(es) of the Regulations (or pursuing them to a proper conclusion, before the contract was entered into)

   d. the breach has affected the chances of the economic operator obtaining the contract.

In respect of the Alstom case and Ground 1:
Alstom argued that no notice had been or could have been served or published: the contract entered into was materially different from that on which the original tender was based and so warranted a new notice and thereby a new tender process.

Eurostar argued that a Contract Notice was not required as they had employed a pre-qualification procedure and that this procedure had been invoked subsequent to an appropriate advisory Notice.

Whilst the court rejected the first of Siemens' arguments, it did not uphold Alstom's case in this respect because the Notice that Siemens had issued sufficed under the wording of the Regulations.

In respect of Ground 2:
Eurostar countered that Alstom had not claimed that they had been prevented from issuing timely proceedings (remember – such proceedings *had* been issued in time) or that their chances of securing the contract had been impaired, and the court concurred with this.

The issue of the standstill period is slightly more complex here under Ground 2: Alstom argued that, because the contract was materially changed, the standstill period was not valid. The court ruled that, even if the requirement for a new tender meant that the standstill period afforded was not valid, Alstom's ability to bring timely proceedings meant that the timescales did not prohibit Alstom from bringing timely action: they were not deprived of this opportunity. (This has a hint of *Catch 22* about it).

The court, therefore, did not uphold Alstom's case under Ground 2, either.

The court then looked at the timings – again further complicated by the claim that the contract had materially changed.

Eurostar claimed that the 30 days allowed to bring proceedings for ineffectiveness had been exceeded. Whilst it was agreed that Alstom had been advised of the award of contract on the 3rd or 4th of December, it was disputed when and even if Alstom had been advised of the reasons for their failure to secure the contract. Eurostar argued that reasons had been given at the time of advice regarding contract award, i.e. at the beginning of December. Alstom argued that they had not been given the reasons because:

- Reasons have to be given in a specified format, and this was not done
- There could never be a summary of reasons because the negotiations with Siemens were for a contract different to that which Alstom had tendered for, because it had been changed during the course of the proceedings
- Alstom had not, anyway, been informed why they had failed in relation to the different tender exercise going ahead with Siemens.

The court rejected all of these claims:

- The summary of reasons need be in no particular form, nor complete at time of initial notification
- The reasons provided at notification of proposal to award (Alcatel) are those that emanate at the time of decision to award. The contract is related to the proposed contract that the contracting authority has been advising bidders it intends to enter into as part of the procurement process. The fact that there were changes to the final version of the contract does not automatically mean that there were two separate tender processes. Whilst material changes may mean the contract

may eventually be outside of the scope of the procurement this does not imply there had been two parallel tendering processes in place.

- Even if the contract is materially altered, there is no reason, in actuality, why the relative merits of a winning and losing bid cannot be identified.
- The court was satisfied that the summary of reasons given to Alstom and time of notification was more than adequate and in a suitable format for the purpose.

On the basis of the above, the court concluded that the effective trigger date for commencement of proceedings was, in fact, the 4th December and by dint of this the claim was out of time – by a long way. Thus, even if the reasons for the application were sound, a ruling of ineffectiveness could not be invoked.

As I said earlier, this tale, hefty though it is, is only part of the matter and there were still claims of breach of process to be considered. However, the outcome of this Application hearing was that the contract with Siemens could go ahead unfettered and the only recourse for Alstom was to continue with the suit in the hope of securing damages if their claims were upheld.

The Remedies Directive is a complex piece of legislation, and cases emanating from it will be complicated – as this taster shows. I suggest you look at the grounds in some detail and make sure you do not fall prey...

What this means

> The stringency of the requirements laid down within the Remedies Directive means that claims for ineffectiveness will not be levelled very often

> As a result, there is relatively little case law on which to base procurement practice or pre-judge the outcome of a claim for ineffectiveness

> The grounds that have to be met are quite specific, and ineffectiveness can only be effected in very specific instances, however...

> When the grounds *are* met, the courts have no choice but to render the contract ineffective

> They may defer the imposition of ineffectiveness in order to mitigate any adverse impact on the greater good

> Action has to be brought within 30 days of the claimant knowing, or being in a position to know, of the transgression

> A re-tender will have to ensue

Cases:

- *Alstom Transport v Eurostar International Ltd & Another (Rev 1) [2011] EWHC 1828 (Ch), judgment of 13 July 2011*

CHAPTER 18 – IN-HOUSE BIDS

Legally, what is an in-house service?
An in-house service means a service performed by an organisation (or department) that is a part of the contracting authority and, under the EU Regulations, when work is to be carried out by an in-house organisation it does not need to be tendered on the open market, regardless of its value. Similarly, if a service currently provided by an external operator is to be brought in-house, it does not need to be advertised (although, of course, TUPE will apply).

This is simple enough, except where the definition of an in-house provider is concerned, and that is what we shall look at now. The 2014 Directive[39] (see Chapter 32) is aiming to be more specific regarding the definition of an in-house provider, and this may help reduce the number of cases that arise on the subject, but it is more complex than you would have at first thought: in fact whole theses have been written on it – but not by me.

As an example, if an authority has a Direct Labour Organisation (DLO) – for example, its property repair service is carried out by its own, employed staff), it is in-house, full stop. But where authorities have 'in-house' provisions that become involved in matters outside of the authority, or other organisations also have an operational interest in that 'in-house provision', then it starts to get more complicated, and that is where case law jumps in.

Earlier on we looked at the *Roanne* case, considering issues surrounding development and land deals. In that case the matter of in-house status came up but we left it alone as it was not relevant to that particular Chapter (10). Instead, we shall look at that aspect of the case here.

Jean Auroux and Others v Commune de Roanne
As already explained above, this is generally known as the Roanne Case, and it all started in 2002 when the Municipal Council of

39. Anticipated in 2014 at time of going to print

Roanne (Roanne) in the Loire Region of France authorised the mayor to enter into contract with the Société d'Equipement du Département de la Loire (SEDL) to build a leisure centre in the town.

SEDL was a semi-public development company but was also a contracting authority in its own right by virtue of its municipal status. Hence it was considered to be an in-house organisation. SEDL was to acquire the land, organise the required design competitions, commission studies, undertake construction and generally manage the project. They were to be paid out of funds secured from various incomes arising from the project, including money from the Roanne Municipal Council.

The challenge came from Jean Aroux and others (Aroux) who contended – amongst other things – that the opportunity should have been tendered on the open market. (Incidentally, Mr Aroux and others were members of the Roanne Municipal Council). The question in this regard was: should a tender not have been issued via OJEU when it was in fact 'handed' to SEDL as an 'internal' operator who will go on to tender the work for sub-contract via EU–compliant processes?

The ECJ stated that the only exceptions to the Public Works Directive are those specifically defined within it and there is no such exclusion in the case of awarding contracts to *other* awarding authorities[40].

The fact that SEDL would have used EU procedures for its own tendering exercises is not relevant.

The fact that SEDL was part of the Département de Loire is irrelevant: only if 'SEDL' had been an internal part of the Municipal Council of Roanne itself could a direct award have been made.

---

40. Some exceptions do exist: where there is an exclusive right in place and where the purchase is via a central purchasing body – but neither of those is relevant here, nor are they in most cases.

In UK speak, if a County Council wants to award a contract to the DLO of a City Council, it cannot do it – the City DLO will have to tender for the work as part of an open competition, just like anyone else. The theoretical County Council can only directly award the work to *its own* DLO.

Roanne was a relatively straightforward in-house/not in-house case for us to cut our teeth on. *The* standard case, and the one by which the principles are currently defined, is that of *Teckal* and hence the right to directly award a contract to an in-house provider has become known as the *Teckal* Exemption. Let us look at *Teckal* now.

Teckal Srl v Comune de Viano and Asienda Gas-Acqua Consorziale (AGAC) di Reggio Emilia

In May of 1997 the Municipality of Viano in Italy directly awarded a contract for heating services and fuel supply to AGAC on the basis that AGAC was a consortium organisation made up of 45 municipalities, of which Viano was one with a share holding of 0.9%.

AGAC was responsible for a number of public services: it had a legal identity, operational autonomy and had to return a profit.

Teckal challenged the direct award and raised the question of whether the award could be made direct to an entity of which the contracting authority is an owner, or whether a public tendering exercise has to be undertaken.

The matter was referred to the ECJ for guidance.

It was decided that, as Viano and AGAC were different legal entities, a tender process should have been undertaken, particularly as the contracts were of financial benefit to the provider. In fact, the ECJ stated that it may even be that contracts might not be directly awarded between different departments within the same authority, depending on the legal structure.

However, the case made it clear that some definitions were required to provide guidance on when a public procurement exercise need not be undertaken – the Teckal exemption. The ECJ stated: "The position can be otherwise (i.e. an EU procurement need not be undertaken) *only* in the case where the local authority exercises over the person concerned a *control* which is similar to that which it exercises over its own departments and, at the same time, that person carries out the essential part of its *activities* with the controlling local authority or authorities".

The definition served to allow the Teckal exemption to apply to a wider range of bodies than had been anticipated – the criteria, if you study them, are fairly relaxed. In fact, it is notable that the judgement itself gave no clear steer on interpreting the guidance it had laid down (for example – what is 'control'? How similar is 'similar'? What constitutes an 'essential part'?).

So, whilst the judgement seems straightforward on the face of it, there have been many cases since that have tested this definition. The new Directives (scheduled for late-2014) are aiming to lay down more stringent criteria for the Teckal 'test' – and these may be employed by courts in advance of that date – but until then, case law is all we have to guide us and Teckal is in the vanguard of these. But there are others. *Stadt Halle* is a well-known example that helped 'tweak' the definition.

Stadt Halle v TREA Leuna
The City of Halle (Halle) had directly commissioned a company called RPL Lochau (Lochau) to draw up plans for a waste disposal plant. TREA Luna (TREA) complained that such a direct award was a breach of EU Regulations in that the contract should have been tendered as an open opportunity across the EU.

In considering whether the commissioning process of the design was exempt from tendering, the ECJ observed that preliminary considerations of an authority's ideas – early planning, if you like – can be tantamount to industry consultation or sounding out the market and so no open tender would be required. Only once the 'discussions' start leading to a legal obligation or contract can it be considered that a tender might be required.

On the issue of whether a contract could have been awarded direct to Lochau, the court opined that, as there was an element of private ownership in Lochau, the Authority could not have the same absolute level of control as it would over an internal organisation and therefore the Teckal exemption did not apply.

Halle had a 75.1% holding in Lochau – a sound majority stake – but it was still just a majority stake, which is not the same as having complete control. The ECJ laid down that even a minority private holding in a company is sufficient to wrest overall control from the contracting authority and so an EU tender would have to be undertaken prior to any contract award.

Once again, I notice that the ECJ is quite clear on the issue, but still does not offer any strict guidance or threshold – 'even a minority private holding' (my quote marks) is not very specific, not in terms of law. In reality, there can be no degree of private holding.

The more recent Brent case helped refine it further.

LB Brent and LB Harrow v Risk Management Partners Limited
London Authorities Mutual Ltd (LAML) was established as a mutual insurance 'society' in order to reduce insurance costs by eliminating the commercial element from the premiums.

In 2007, LB Brent (Brent) tendered for various insurance services but withdrew the tender and instead, on the basis of the now-established Teckal exemption, awarded the contract to LAML. Risk Management Partners Ltd (RMP), who had originally tendered for the work, challenged the decision on the basis that the work should have been tendered on the open market, and four areas of breach were considered:

1. Does Teckal apply to the 2006 Regulations (i.e. the UK jurisdiction)
2. Does Teckal apply to contracts of insurance?
3. Must the local authority have absolute control over the contracting body, or can it be part of a collective level of control?
4. If being part of a collective level of control is OK, was the level of control specifically held by Brent in the instance of LAML sufficient?

Cutting a long story short, the High Court supported the challenge, as did the Court of Appeal, but the LB Harrow went on to appeal to the Supreme Court who unanimously allowed the appeal on the following grounds:

1. Teckal does apply to the EU Regulations 2006 because it is "a significant and policy-based exemption" so must apply across all member states, and the 2006 Regulations interpret the EU procurement regulations for UK law.
2. The Supreme Court stated it was immaterial that the contract was between two distinct bodies (i.e. that providing insurance services is nothing like the work that local authorities do) but it is rather a question of where does the requisite degree of control over the service provider lay. Thus, on point (2) in isolation, Teckal will apply.
3. This point was more crucial. The set-up of LAML decreed that [a] if a member's insurance claim was being considered, they were excluded from the Board's discussions and [b] the Board had the power to terminate an authority's membership if they so wished. On this basis, control was absolutely collective and not individually held by any one member body. So is collective influence adequate to satisfy Teckal? The Court held that 'decisive influence' – as required – is possible, albeit any member is part of a collective decision-making body, and such

collaboration is consistent with the EU's procurement rules and in the public interest.

4. So, if collective influence is OK, did Brent have sufficient control to meet the Teckal criterion? The Court noted that no Board meeting was quorate unless the majority of the directors present represented a participating member of LAML, and participating members had 100% of the Board voting rights. On this basis, the Teckal criterion raised in point (4) was met.

On these bases, Brent was able to appoint directly.

These four cases have helped shape the issue of appointing in-house providers – a more complex area than might at first have been thought. We now wait to see what the 2014 Directive brings.

What this means

> The EU Regulations state that the award of a contract to an in-house bidder or organisation requires no tender process

> On the face of it, what is and what isn't an in-house service seems obvious but this is not always the case

> With more and more public organisations seeking to find economies through sharing services, and with the insource/ outsource argument raising its head again, the edges can become quite blurred

> To determine if an organisation is an in-house provision, you need to assess whether the Teckal Exemption applies, namely:
> > ✔ The service provider carries out the principal part of its activities with the relevant public body.
> > ✔ The public body exercises the same kind of control over the service provider as it does over its own departments.
> > ✔ There is no private sector ownership of the service provider or any intention that there should be any

Cases:

- *Jean Auroux and Others v Commune de Roanne, Case C-220/05, judgment of 18 January 2007*
- *Teckal Srl v Comune de Viano and Asienda Gas-Acqua Consorziale (AGAC) di Reggio Emilia (C-107/98) 1999 ECR-I-8121.*
- *Stadt Halle v TREA Leuna , Case C-26/03 judgment of 11 January 2005.*
- *Brent London Borough Council and Harrow London Borough Council v Risk Management Partners Limited [2011] UKSC 7.*

CHAPTER 19 – LATE SUBMISSIONS

Dealing with late submissions is not always as straightforward as it may seem.

PQQ and tender return dates and times are sacrosanct. There are few justifiable reasons for changing them[41] and these can normally be clearly identified – for example because of a *force majeure*. As always, there is case law that shows some of the quirks around this issue and demonstrates how fuzzy the reasoning can sometimes be.

The case of *Leadbitter* is one such example.

J B Leadbitter & Co Ltd v Devon County Council
The tender concerned was for a construction framework with a submission deadline for electronic submissions of 12.00 noon on 16th January 2009. One of the bidders (Apollo) suffered a power failure at the crucial moment and so the deadline was extended for all bidders to 3.00pm, and confirmed to them all by e-mail at 11.13am (the timings are, of course, critical in this matter).

The ITT stated that tender submissions had to include 4 case studies and that, because the submission deadline was strict and all documents had to be submitted at the same time, bidders should be careful to allow sufficient time to upload their submissions[42].

Leadbitter submitted their bid by 12.05pm on the due day – within the extended deadline – but at 2.45pm realised the four case studies had been omitted. They were unable to add these to the already-submitted tender as the portal would not allow it (all documents had to be submitted at the same time). At 2.59pm (plus 30 seconds!) Leadbitter spoke to the lead procurement officer at Devon and finally submitted the missing case studies at 3.26pm.

41. The only consideration, of course, is to extend them
42. This is – or should be - a standard caution in any ITT where any form of electronic submission is involved. It is sensible advice, of course, but also protects the contracting organisation if there is a problem with submitting the bids due to slow systems, etc., so you are advised to include a paragraph to this effect.

Was the bid acceptable?

Because we are looking at the case here, you can guess that the Council (Devon) rejected the bid on the grounds that an incomplete submission had been made, but were they right[43]? Would you have done the same?

Leadbitter brought an action through the High Court with an injunction seeking either a consideration of its bid or damages in consideration of work it might have secured through the framework. The case was based on three claimed counts of where Devon had not met its obligations under the EU Procurement Regulations by:

1. Not treating all bidders equally and non-discriminatorily
2. Not acting proportionately
3. Not selecting contractors on the basis of MEAT criteria.

I thought this last one was an interesting claim. What did the court think?

Bearing in mind the timings and the fact that there had been a submission error identified before the amended tender submission deadline, the Court agreed that there were grounds for the case to be heard and on each of the three claims in turn, the court found as follows.

1. Not treating all bidders equally and non-discriminatorily.
In the matter of not treating all bidders equally and non-discriminatorily, Leadbitter claimed two concessions by Devon to other bidders meant that they had not been treated equally:

- Devon had allowed an extension of time when Apollo suffered a power cut but not when Leadbitter had omitted their case studies. The court decided that these were not similar circumstances in that the problems experienced by Apollo were outside of their control. It could be argued that Apollo should

---

43. Remember – this is a legal issue, not a moral one.

not have left it so late to load the documents but it transpired that of 24 submissions, 16 were also left until the last minute and Leadbitter themselves took advantage of the extension.

A point of my own on this is that (a) bidders will always tend to leave it to the last minute, no matter how long you give them and (b) if the deadline is 12.00pm, there is nothing legally or technically wrong with uploading a bid at 11.50am, for example, or delivering it at 11.58am. It may be unwise or risky, but nothing more than that. If you leave it late and fail to make the deadline, that is your fault, and it is silly, but it is not against any rules.

- Devon had allowed a bidder (Midas) to submit back-up hard copies of their case studies because they had had rung up at 10.30am on the day of the submission to say they were not sure they had uploaded properly. Of course, this could not be checked until after the submission deadline and anyway the system did not allow more than one upload (Leadbitter's problem). The back-up copies were submitted in a sealed package before the tender deadline.

  Of course, this 'allowance' on the part of Devon was spurious – it did not comply with the requirements of the ITT and was made without any legal back-up or advice. As it happens, this issue was not put to the test as the Midas bid was complete without recourse to even looking at the hard copies. Leadbitter had not submitted any back-up copies prior to the deadline but had e-mailed copies (despite e-mailed submissions being unacceptable) after the deadline[44].

So, for Leadbitter, the Midas 'concession' was not realised and so could not be used as an argument.

Leadbitter raised one more issue, claiming it had not been allowed

---

44. Had they done so, the question of acceptability and compliance with ITT requirements still prevails, but this, too, was never tested.

to correct errors in a bid that had been submitted before the tender deadline, as the terms of the ITT had allowed. The Court rejected this outright, saying that the rejection was on the grounds of incompleteness, not errors.

The Court also pointed out that the fact that documents all had to be uploaded at one time, and that supplementary uploads were not possible, made it clear that any omissions in the submissions could not be corrected. Fax and e-mail submissions were unacceptable and these terms and conditions of tendering equally applied to all bidders.

2. Not acting proportionately.

On the matter of not acting proportionately, Leadbitter claimed the rejection of their bid was disproportionate to the issue of an omission of a document. The issue of proportionality is an odd one and, whilst legal claims of disproportionality have been upheld in courts, the principle still puzzles a lot of people. We will look at proportionality in Chapter 24, but the Court's observations in this case are interesting:

- The submission process was clearly defined in the ITT documentation: any deviation from this could have left Devon open to challenges of unequal treatment, discrimination and lack of transparency – the three golden rules of EU procurement. Deviation from the rules (by either party) is not a good idea and requires very sure grounds for it to even be considered.
- Whilst Leadbitter did not offer a submission of the missing case studies by e-mail, this would not have been acceptable anyway as the 'package' would not have been secure.
- Devon, as the Contracting Authority, had laid down the submission rules and could, in theory, waive them as it saw fit, but to do so would provide advantage to the benefitting bidder – for example, accepting a late bid allows that tenderer extra time not made available to other bidders – and such a waiver could potentially be employed to favour preferred bidders.
- Conversely, the Court recognised that Leadbitter had submitted

their bid on time and that the case studies were prepared in good time – their omission was purely a technical error. Allowing the supplementary submission of the case studies would not necessarily have disadvantaged any of the other bidders and on this basis, Leadbitter's Claim was 'strong'. However...

*   The 'rules' of the ITT were clear – there was only an opportunity for a single upload and late submissions would not be accepted. Devon was well within its rights to reject the bid and on this basis, there was not an issue of disproportionality.

My view, at this point, is to note how important it is to make your conditions of tender submission absolutely clear, and make it plain what is and what is not acceptable. Another useful caveat is reserving the right to reject – if you are not careful, being too emphatic can paint you into a corner where you are obliged to do what you actually do not want to do. Always look at the 'what ifs....'

3.   Not selecting contractors on the basis of MEAT criteria.
Leadbitter claimed contravention of the rules by not selecting contractors on the basis of MEAT criteria in that, by rejecting their bid, Devon had precluded the opportunity of considering a bid which, in reality, had the potential to most effectively meet the award criteria.

The Court rejected this, saying that, as part of any procurement process, bids may be rejected on the grounds of non-compliance. These bids may have otherwise been successful, but that is not the point: they were not acceptable and so do not enter into the equation. The consideration is whether the rules have been applied in a way which is – yes – equitable, transparent and non-discriminatory. Provided those criteria are met, a rejection cannot, in general, be contested.

From a seemingly minor error, a whole host of issues arose so be clear of your ITT 'rules of engagement' and make sure they are clear to the bidders and suitable for you and your organisation: you need to stick to them so they have to be right and they have to be clear.

What this means

The arguments in this matter are similar to those raised in the chapter on errors and omissions (Chapter 14). The lessons to be learned are therefore much the same:

> Unless the lateness of a submission is your fault, in law you cannot accept a late bid – because that would be prejudicial to the fair treatment of the other bidders who submitted on time

> Regardless, the rules on submission cited in the ITT must be upheld and applied equitably to all parties

---

Cases:

• *J B Leadbitter & Co Ltd v Devon County Council ([2009] EWHC 930 (Ch)), judgment of 01 May 2009*

CHAPTER 20 – LIQUIDATED & ASCERTAINED DAMAGES

What exactly are Liquidated and Ascertained Damages?
Liquidated and Ascertained Damages (LADs) tend to be used a lot in (but are by no means limited to) the construction sector. They comprise specified levels of compensation (or damages) payable as cash (i.e. liquidated) if and when an identified (i.e. ascertainable) event has occurred such as will cause the client a loss, all in accordance with specifics laid down in the contract.

A 'construction world' example of such a warranty would be where major repairs were being undertaken to premises awaiting re-let. The contract would have a completion date written in and failure to meet that date would cause the client to lose rental income. This loss is recoverable as damages (LADs) but when laying down such terms in a contract there are some criteria that have to be observed:

a. the formula by which such losses are calculated must be declared quite clearly and specifically in the contract and
b. the losses must be tangible and 'showable' and
c. they must be 'expressable' in terms of cash loss

The main drawback is that sometimes such losses are hard to predict and you cannot add bits in later, but some contracts really need to have such clauses in them to ensure or 'encourage', so far as is possible, that a contract, for example, completes on time or otherwise delivers what it is supposed to.

Dunlop Pneumatic Tyre Co Ltd v New Garage & Motor Co Ltd
Long ago as it was (1915) the Case of Dunlop Pneumatic Tyre Co Ltd (Dunlop) v New Garage & Motor Co Ltd (New Garage) was a landmark case in that it set clear parameters for LADs which are still used as the acid test today.

New Garage signed an Agreement with Dunlop for the retailing of their products. Clause 5 of this Agreement stated *"We agree to pay to the Dunlop Pneumatic Tyre Company, Ltd. the sum of £5 for each and every tyre, cover or tube sold or offered in breach of this agreement, as and by way of liquidated damages and not as a penalty."* Of course (otherwise the case would not be in this book) New Garage broke this condition and Dunlop claimed Liquidated Damages.

I will not labour the case itself any further (you can always look it up yourself) save to say that out of the proceedings came four tests that are still applied today to see if the damages claimed are valid as LADs, that is, it needs to be asked, in turn, if the sums claimed:

a. Are described as a penalty
b. Are *not* described as a penalty
c. Are a true estimate of damages formed in advance, i.e. at the time of contract
d. Are not payable on all breaches of contract.

Looking at these in turn, Courts will not impose penalties so anything described as such will be out of the door straight away. Also, a sum will be a penalty, even if not described as one, if:

i. The amount claimed is *"extravagant and unconscionable in amount compared to the greatest loss that would have resulted from the breach"*[45] i.e. an extortionate sum
ii. Where the breach is a failure to pay a sum of money that is less than the LAD sum, the LAD will be deemed a penalty.

These two points reinforce the principle of a*scertained* damages.

If the sums claimed (often referred to as 'stipulated sums') are not deemed to be a penalty, then tests (c) and (d) kick in: the sums cited in the contract must be a true and realistic estimate of damages if the named breach/es occur and the sums quoted must not be payable in the case of all or any breach (i.e. LADs must

---

45.Lord Dunedin quoting from an earlier case on a similar issue.

not be a cover-all 'damage' – that would bring it back to being a penalty).

All this means that LADs must be estimated and set in the contract as a true estimate of costs or losses if a specified breach occurs. In construction, a commonly-named breach is late completion when rent losses in a building may occur but, as the Dunlop Case shows, the losses do not have to be rent and it does not have to apply to construction. The point is, the losses must be identified as the actual costs and losses the client would incur as a result of a specific breach. In practice, you could have several of these in one contract.

The corollary or upshot of this is that the claims cannot be levied against any breach other than that identified against the stipulated sums in the contract.

In practice, this makes LADs fair to both parties. The client is obviously covered and the contractor has agreed the level of damages by virtue of signing up to the contract and is then protected by the limit set by the formula. The contractor has certainty of potential claims, knows the impact of the risk and can allow for this in the tender, if it is felt necessary.

Interestingly, the client does not have to prove the actual losses amount to the level set by the LAD formula. The settlement is contractual, so no argument can be levelled and, as a result, costly legal actions are avoided. In our pretend example above: the work finished late – you have to pay it. Simple.

So, when preparing your tender and contract documents, do not include penalties – that is a legal no-no. Any losses you can foresee arising from a breach need to be named and calculated. This is often difficult, but regardless – if you want to claim them you will have to lay it out plain and clear and declare the formula you have used. Or you can rely on a costly court action.

Guarantees

Guarantees are somewhat more difficult to explain insofar as they are really so akin to a Performance Bond that there is little daylight between them. My personal view is that a guarantee can be used to warranty a specific part of a contract or performance within it, and may be offered by the provider themselves, whilst a Bond is more often specifically designed to cover the eventuality of the provider failing to complete the contract due to their untimely demise and is always underwritten by a third party.

What this means

> You can claim losses and damages (LADs) but you cannot impose penalties

> LADs have to be calculated according to a formula declared at time of tender

> The default event itself prompts the imposition of LADs: proof of actual loss is not required

> Odd though this may seem, the methodology protects both client and contractor

---

Cases:

• *Dunlop Pneumatic Tyre Co Ltd v New Garage & Motor Co Ltd [1914] UKHL 1 (01 July 1914)*

CHAPTER 21 – MISTAKES & MISUNDERSTANDINGS

The context of this chapter

My main considerations will relate to contractual misunderstandings. A first thought might be that contractual misunderstandings are not anything to do with procurement, but in fact getting the contract right is relevant to procurement: we want people knowing what they are bidding for. So we will have a quick look at this and try and learn from some examples.

I have used the term misunderstanding, but in law the term is 'mistake' – erroneous content or an erroneous conception of intent (by the other party). Of course, it is not as simple as that when the matter comes to court and the law views mistakes as being any one of three distinct types:

- Common
- Mutual
- Unilateral

Each of these can, in turn, be a mistake of fact or a mistake of law, and a court will consider each type in a different way, but always it will consider them in the context of the present not the future[46].

- *Common Mistake*

In this instance, 'common' means common to both parties in that both parties to the contract are equally mistaken in their belief. As it happens, case law has done little to help predict the stand a court will take on a matter such as this. We will look at a couple of instances.

Bell v Lever Bros and Solle v Butcher

Bell was a case in the House of Lords where the judgement is still relied on today, stating that a Common Mistake must "*relate to something which both parties must necessarily have accepted*

46. An odd phrase – read on to see what it means in practice

in their minds as an essential element of the subject matter." If a common misunderstanding is fundamental to the contract – for example, an agreement for the use of a building which, it is later discovered, has collapsed – then the courts can set the contract aside.

Solle extended this 'definition' to the point where a contract enforceable in law could be voided if the circumstances were appropriate. A case in 2002 tested both of these rulings. Let's look at it.

Great Peace Shipping Ltd v Tsavliris Salvage International Ltd
Great Peace Shipping Ltd (GP) chartered a ship (the 'Great Pease') to Tsavliris Salvage International Ltd (Tsavliris) to provide salvage and support services to another vessel. Both parties believed the two ships were close to each other whilst in fact they were 400 miles apart (not far in a Tornado jet, perhaps, but quite a distance if you are to provide support by sea). The error was not discovered until after the contract had been concluded (signed).

In the event, another ship provided the required assistance and so the services intended to be provided by GP were cancelled. GP sought payment and Tsavliris refused on the basis that the contract was void due to a common mistake in fact and one that allowed Tsavliris to rescind the contract in that, although the contract *could* have been enforced legally, there was a common mistake or misunderstanding that rendered the contract unworkable (my phrasing). It seems Tsavliris felt that if *Bell* did not work, then *Solle* would.

In fact, the court found in favour of GP on the basis that the 400-plus mile separation of the two vessels (as opposed to the 35 miles the parties thought it was) did not render the provision of the contracted service impossible to deliver. Slower – yes. Impossible, no.

In reaching this decision, the court recognised the Bell and Solle cases and actually stated, in so many words, that they did not help each other in clarifying such matters, in fact they contradicted each other. On balance, the court came down against *Solle* in that it was felt you could not rescind a contract that was deliverable *in law*. Remember that – 'in law' (my quotes).

One last point of note the court made on the process of deciding such cases was to consider if whether, in making the contract, either party took on any element of the risk the agreement might present. We always consider apportionment of risk as part of a procurement process but not often to the point where it may be considered the contract is undeliverable. Maybe we should.

- *Mutual Mistake*

Subtly different from Common Mistake, a Mutual Mistake is one where the two parties genuinely misunderstand each other and, despite good intent, are at total cross purposes. The Raffles case is a well-known instance.

Raffles v Wichelhaus

This is another old case (1864) which still stands. The contract was for the sale of a cargo of cotton from Bombay (now Mumbai) aboard a ship named 'The Peerless'. All fine, so far, except that there were *two* ships called 'The Peerless' set to sail from Mumbai with cotton, but at different times – one in October, the other in December. Raffles thought he had bought the December cargo whilst Wichelhaus was convinced it was the October shipment.

The court decided that the transaction or contract was ambiguous to the point where it was not valid and could not stand.

It is easy with the wisdom of hindsight to say that such an error was careless – why, for instance, was the shipment not more specifically defined? Or, would the anticipated delivery date not have given the game away? Maybe, of course, but that is the whole point: mistakes can happen and we have a duty of care to try and avoid them. Be clear; be specific. In a phrase: be pedantic.

- *Unilateral Mistake*

A unilateral mistake is one made by one party that was known or recognised by the other party – or *should* have been known or recognised by the other party – but which was not raised as an issue at time of contract.

Where this is clearly the case, and a true error occurs, the contract may be declared void by the court. However, this line of thought may not be followed if the error was due to lack of judgement: a distinction is drawn between a genuine error and (perhaps) mere lack of competence. This approach is also based on quite old case law and a court's distinction in a case between the two trains of thought is not overly easy to predict. The following, more recent case illustrates that it can get even foggier.

Statoil ASA v Louis Dreyfus Energy Services

The case concerned an agreement about levels of demurrage or compensation payable for delays caused to the unloading of a ship. Statoil had made an error in the calculation of values and Louis Dreyfus Energy Services (Dreyfus) spotted it but did not point it out. Statoil sought to rescind the contract but the court declined.

Basing the judgement on other cases, the court stated that, just because a mistake is made regarding a fact on which the contract is based, if that fact does not actually form a part of the contract then the contract has to stand.

The court can take a different view if a mistake – in fact or law - leads to an unintended outcome.

Gibbon v Mitchell

In this case a contract was annulled because it was agreed that a mistake had led to the contract not having the effect that was intended. In the judge's[47] summing up, he said:

---

47. Justice Millet

"...wherever there is a voluntary transaction by which one party intends to confer bounty to another, the deed will be set aside if the court is satisfied that the disponor[48] did not intend the transaction to have the effect which it did. It will be set aside for mistake whether the mistake is a mistake of law or of fact, so long as the mistake is as to the effect of the transaction itself and not merely as to its consequences or the advantages to be gained by entering into it."

This is not an easy paragraph to understand (unless you are a lawyer) but the principle is often employed in cases of mistake – for example in the relatively recent case of *Andrew Fender v National Westminster Bank PLC*, which follows.

Andrew Fender (Administrator of FG Collier & Sons Ltd.) v National Westminster Bank PLC
In this case, the bank allowed the release of a holding or lien on a property, mistakenly believing that the debt to which it related had been cleared.

The court set aside the deed on the basis that it would have turned the bank into an unsecured creditor, which was clearly not the intention of the release.

Some overall conclusions.

1. These examples demonstrate that mistakes in contracts are a reality, and have been made by people much better (you may think) than ourselves. We must be aware that we and our colleagues can also make mistakes in contracts – or other documents. Checking and proof-reading is essential because a correction or solution through law may not bring the outcome you want.
2. Strenuously avoid any ambiguity or potential misunderstanding in documentation. This chapter refers to contracts but we have seen in earlier chapters that lack of clarity in tender documents

---

48. In this instance, disponor means the person making the error

can also be an issue. Have people check that your intentions are clearly stated, and do use plain language.

One final point on contracts: in common law a contract may be rescinded or annulled if there is a mistake in the identification of a party to the contract. An example may be where a person deliberately provides a false identity when signing up to an agreement in order to commit fraud.

I do not suppose you will encounter this professionally (at least in the context of this book) but I thought I'd let you know.

Misunderstandings at procurement stage
There are examples throughout this book where challenges are levelled on the grounds of ambiguity, misunderstanding or misleading information, and these will become clearer as you read on. I will, however, put the issue into procurement context by looking at one particular case where the issue of clarity in tendering instructions was paramount to the challenge. The case itself was extremely complex and the detail far too involved to be covered in any depth here but I will share with you the judges' comments on the issue of clarity in tendering instructions because I think it throws some light and common sense on the matter.

Clinton (t/a Oriel Training Services) v Department for Employment and Learning & Another
Clinton challenged the Department for Employment and Learning & Another (DEL) primarily on their decision to reject Clinton's tender submission to provide training and apprenticeship programmes in Northern Ireland on the grounds that it had insufficient evidence to support key elements of the bid.

The basis of the challenge was that Clinton thought they had submitted sufficient information and so claimed the tender requirements were ambiguous. The High Court upheld this view and so found in favour of Clinton. DEL went to Appeal and, by a majority of 2 to 1, the Appeal Court upheld the High Court's findings and the Appeal was dismissed. It was a protracted affair.

What I am most interested in are the words of the High Court Judges in this case, commenting on what contracting authorities ought to expect of bidders in their ability to comprehend instructions and explanations.

I will quote the relevant excerpts, as I think they are self-explanatory.

Justice McCloskey stated that any evaluation criterion should be formulated in accordance with what has become known as the 'Siac'[49] test, i.e. written *"...in such a way as to allow all reasonably well informed and normally diligent tenderers to interpret it in the same way."*

It was noted that the terms 'reasonable' and 'normal' allowed the tenderer a degree of latitude for error, inattention and *"other human weakness"*, in other words, despite putting the onus on the bidder to comprehend, the degree of clarity must be adequate to allow for human traits.

Justice McCloskey went on to say (and this is my favourite bit) *"... the Siac hypothetical tenderer is a terrestrial, rather than celestial, being, hailing from earth and not heaven. In its determination of this issue, I consider that the court should approach the matter not as an exercise in statutory construction or as one involving the interpretation of a deed or contract or other legal instrument..."* and went on to say that contracting authorities must remember that bidders are people from industry, not lawyers.

In these words it is writ clear: when writing tender documents and in particular with regard to evaluation criteria (the touchiest area):

• Use clear, plain, English

---

49. The Siac Test comes from *SIAC Construction v Mayo County Council*[Case C-19/00] [2002] All ER (EC) 272

- Ask colleagues to say what they think you mean by what you have written
- Don't try and be smart – keep it as simple as you can (you are not trying to prove anything about yourself)
- Do not be afraid to repeat your requirements, albeit in a different way, to meet the different 'human traits' you may encounter in a range of bidders.
- Examples and models always help, so do not be afraid to use them – but make it clear that they are examples or models and not a hint or guide to the required answer.

What this means

> Mistakes and misunderstandings can easily occur and can have serious consequences

> They can occur in tender documents as well as contract clauses

> Ensure that what is being signed up to is patently clear and do not be afraid to be tautological[50]

> Have a critical friend check the apparent meaning and context of what you have written – does it pass the SIAC test?

> Where a misunderstanding has occurred, check the type (in law) of the misunderstanding to gauge the outcome of any potential legal action so as to better-prepare your mitigation

---

Cases:

- *Bell v Lever Bros [1932] AC 161*
- *Solle v Butcher ([1950] 1KB 671)*

---

50. Tautology: defined as "repetition of the same sense in different words". Do not be afraid to do this if it serves to define and avoid confusion.

- *Great Peace Shipping Ltd v Tsavliris Salvage International Ltd [2002] EWCA Civ 1407.*
- *Raffles v Wichelhaus [1864] 2 H & C 906*
- *Statoil ASA v Louis Dreyfus Energy Services LP [2008] EWHC 2257 (Comm)*
- *Gibbon v Mitchell [1990] 1 WLR 1304*
- *Andrew Fender (Administrator of FG Collier & Sons Ltd.) v National Westminster Bank PLC [2008] EWHC 2242*
- *Clinton (t/a Oriel Training Services) v Department for Employment and Learning & Another ([2012] NICA 48). judgment of 13 November 2012*

CHAPTER 22 – PRE-TENDER DIALOGUE

What is pre-tender dialogue?

The adage 'if you want to know something, ask the people who do it'[51] is particularly appropriate to procurement, where you are often asked to source something about which you have little – if any - knowledge. The solution lies, of course, within the project team, which must include the experts and specialists you need.

However, one source of expertise often overlooked is the providers themselves: who could know better? Pre-tender dialogue may be better known as industry consultation and comprises seeking views from the industry on your proposals and getting feedback on any aspects of it. You may wish to have advice on the specification or your proposals for the tender process and seeking the views of the industry is perfectly legitimate, although there are, of course, pitfalls.

There is always a risk of accusations of collusion, particularly if the company you consulted wins the bid and *especially* if they happen to be the incumbent as well. Of course this can be avoided through consulting with several companies, not revealing anything singularly helpful to any one company and doubling up on your efforts to demonstrate equality of opportunity and impartiality.

As I always say – the intention is always to avoid challenge, but if one arises, you need to be able to prove good process, so be prepared.

Most of this you may well already know, so let us move on quickly to look at an example that has been through the courts and which is quite definitive, if not a little odd.

Fabricom SA v Belgian State

This is the key case on the issue of whether a person or company who has assisted at the preparatory stage of a tender may participate in it and iterates the EU laws relating to this matter.

---

51. My adage.

The case was triggered by a law in Belgium under the procurement legislation regarding the time for which a person who had worked on a tender was prohibited from participating in it (although a firm they are connected with may be allowed)[52].

Fabricom lodged appeals against this law, claiming it contravened (amongst other things) the EU requirement for equality of opportunity and proportionality, and the Human Rights Act as well (presumably for good measure).

The Belgian Conseil d'État referred the matter to the ECJ seeking advice on whether or not the Belgian law was contrary to (then) EC public procurement directives.

The ECJ stated that the Directives concerned are designed to ensure competition and that equality of opportunity is of paramount importance to this. They went on to say that this means (by definition) that similar situations cannot be treated differently and different situations cannot be treated similarly. This may sound a bit prosaic, but actually it is a help in understanding how the ECJ reached its decision.

The ECJ stated:

- Someone who has been involved in work preparatory to a tender is not necessarily in the same position with regards to tendering as others who have not been involved
- That person may have certain advantages by virtue of their prior involvement.
- There may be a conflict of interest in that their involvement may have had the effect, albeit unintentionally, of influencing the conditions of the tender or contract in a manner that favoured them.
- Any of these could distort competition between tenderers.

From this stems the conclusion that a person who has been

---

52. The actual wording is slightly more convoluted than that, but that is the gist of it.

involved in the early stages of a tender should not necessarily be treated in the same way as someone who hasn't. Now the 'prosaic' sentence we looked at earlier begins to make some sense...

Here is the twist – a rule that forbids a person who has prior involvement from participating in the tender gives them no chance to demonstrate that they had no competitive advantage, and this would be disproportionate to the aim of ensuring equal treatment. It is almost like *Catch 22* (which is not covered here).

Accordingly, the Directives do not allow you to automatically rule out of the tender process anyone who has provided assistance in the preparatory stages if they have not been afforded the chance to prove they have gained no unfair advantage. It goes strangely further than that:

A contracting authority may not consider whether a bidder in such a position is eligible to partake in the procurement until after the evaluation process (!)[53] It is considered in law that only when the bids are assessed can any unfair advantage be judged, which is logical, but the delay incurred in reaching a negative decision has impacted on the bidder's rights to challenge. This is contrary to the intentions of the Remedies Directive, which was not intended...

I can make no further comment on this save that, yes: you can have dialogue with potential providers and allow them to bid but you must ensure the tendering playing field is level or it can get messy.

What this means

> Never be afraid to hold pre-tender dialogue – it is good to ask the people who know and often silly not to

---

53. Remedies Directive.

> Be open about it – ask more than one provider and remember an 'event[54]' is always a good idea

> Take care to evaluate all submissions according to an even playing field

> Paying a provider (e.g. an incumbent) for pre-tender advice and input (as you would a consultant, for example) can often allay any misunderstanding that a consideration for these services will be effected at the tender evaluation stage

> Make sure the tender process is transparent and well documented. This is always required, of course, but it is particularly important when a bidder who was involved in pre-tender dialogue is successful and a challenge is levelled on the grounds that they consequently received favourable treatment. The winner must *always* win it fair and square

---

Cases:

* *Fabricom SA v Belgian State, judgment of 3 March 2005, Cases C-21/03 and C-34/03*

---

54. An 'event' means just that – where providers in the market are invited to learn about the opportunity and give feedback on the proposals. Market interest can be accurately judged at such events.

CHAPTER 23 – PROCESS & PROCESS ERRORS

What Do We Mean by Process?
Process includes all the things we do in a procurement, so it is natural that issues arising under this heading will cross several boundaries. This first case does that but it is still a good illustration of a process error in particular and how the courts may choose to address such an instance.

Mears Ltd v Leeds City Council
In October 2009 Leeds City Council (Leeds) tendered for improvement and repair works to its social housing stock using the Competitive Dialogue Process. Mears were successful at PQQ and proceeded through to the ITPD[55] stage.

The ITPD required Outline Solutions and during the course of this stage some changes were issued to the pricing and quality aspects of the required submission. After the Outline Solutions had been submitted Leeds issued a clarification and asked for some revised information on the submissions pricing aspect.

About six weeks later, Mears received notice that they had been unsuccessful at the ITPD stage and would not be invited forwards to the ITCD[56] stage.

Mears reacted by, in October, issuing proceedings seeking suspension of the process and an order that Leeds either re-run the process in its entirety or from the ITPD stage.

The grounds for this suit were essentially that Leeds had:

- breached the 2006 Regulations in that they
- failed to act transparently and/or treat Mears equally and in a non-discriminatory manner,

55. ITPD – Invitation to Participate in Dialogue
56. ITCD – Invitation to Continue Dialogue

- issued changes during the process and allowed insufficient time for a response and
- evaluated the tenders using undisclosed criteria and weightings.

As part of the hearing process, Leeds agreed not to proceed to award until the matter was settled and presented their model answers to a confidentiality ring[57] for examination. The Court also ruled that the claim regarding the letter for clarification of pricing within the Outline Solution was out of time – albeit the main claim was still within time.

It was accepted that the claim regarding the tender evaluation was within time as Mears would not have known for sure of the situation until disclosure of the model answers to the ring of confidentiality.

It was agreed that the model answers should have been disclosed at time of tender as they were of material importance (my words) to the bidders and contained more than just guidance to the evaluation panel as they conferred scoring, weighting and other similar details to which the bidders should have been party.

The court went on to list a range of disclosure requirements regarding evaluation criteria at tender stage: we have already looked at those in Chapter 9 so we shall not re-visit them but the bottom line is that the court found in favour of Mears and agreed that the process was flawed.

The court had the right to stop the award being made and to have the process re-run. However, it decided not to as this would not have been in the best interests of the residents concerned. Instead, it allowed the award to go ahead and made an award of compensatory damages to Mears.

Thus courts have the right to make a contracting authority undergo a tender process again – provided the circumstances are right – but

---

57. Confidentiality Ring – a limited group of essential persons sworn to confidentiality, usually and primarily the lawyers.

may not always do so, particularly if it is not in the best interests of those concerned overall.

This next one is different – it looks at an issue surrounding CPV[58] Codes.

Ombudsman inquiry into complaint against the European Aviation Safety Agency (EASA)

The litigant or complainant in this instance was a German citizen who worked as an information broker, advising clients of suitable tenders as they came up on the Tenders Electronic Daily (TED) website.

In 2009, EASA advertised an opportunity made up of five various Lots across a range of requirements:

- web applications development and maintenance;
- client-service applications, development and maintenance;
- system data base and network administration;
- maintenance and support;
- content, records and document management implementation, maintenance and support.

EASA placed all of these under one CPV Code: 72000000, which is for IT services: consulting, software development, Internet and support. I don't know about you, but I think that's lazy.

The complainant claimed that the single CPV Code made it difficult for individual suppliers to select their niche within the Lots available. EASA rejected the complaint, saying that the Code issued covered all the requirements adequately and declined to issue a correction.

The Ombudsman stated that the point of the CPV Codes was to describe the requirements as accurately as possible, and to do this across all language barriers. Whilst he accepted that the overarching

---

58. CPV – Common Procurement Vocabulary – you should know this.

code used did cover the general area of supply, it did not accurately define the individual Lots.

The Ombudsman concluded that the use of the one Code, covering as it did some 250 sub codes, did not take adequate account of suppliers' needs when seeking opportunities.

EASA argued that the process was successful as it had received a record number of bids, but the Ombudsman refused to accept that this proved the single code did not serve to disadvantage some potential bidders: the impact of using more appropriately detailed codes would never be known.

The Ombudsman therefore decided it was a case of maladministration but was unable to take any further action as the process had been completed. However, he "expected" EASA to take the criticism into account in future procurements.

The lesson is clear – not just for saving the bother of a complaint or challenge but in principle – always be as specific with your CPV Codes as you can when publishing your OJEU Notice, It *does* make a difference.

What it means

> Good process is fundamental to any procurement exercise; bad process is the most common cause of a legal challenge to the outcome

> Process is easy – why mess it up? There is really little excuse and rarely a successful defence

> Do not be lazy and try to shortcut the exercise – the example of the CPVs above is a prime example of shoddiness due to a lazy approach to the process

> Remember that 'process' includes aspects such as timescales,

transparency, evaluation criteria, weightings and so on, and all of these aspects have clear requirements within the regulations. Adhere to those requirements and your process will be considered good

---

Cases:

- *Mears Ltd v Leeds City Council (No 2) ([2011] EWHC 1031 (TCC)). Judgment of 19 April 2011.*
- *Decision of the European Ombudsman closing his inquiry into complaint 333/2009/(BEH)KM against the European Aviation Safety Agency (EASA)*

CHAPTER 24 – PROPORTIONALITY

What is proportionality?
The concept of proportionality is one that some people find hard to comprehend – even though it is a specific requirement of the EU Treaty. So what is it?

Proportionality is – strangely – keeping a procurement process proportional to the nature of the requirement. In plain language, do not make things more complicated or difficult than they need to be to achieve the desired result.

If you are issuing tenders for the construction of a section of Cross-Rail or the provision of NHS Trust medical services, the tender will be unavoidably complex, due to both the scale and the complexity of the requirement. If, instead, you are tendering for an internal mail delivery service then the tendering process can be much simpler and it would be expected to be so.

What can you fail to keep in proportion? Well, lots of things, at both PQQ and tender stages. Prime candidates for disproportionality are quality evaluation requirements; for example, are you asking 'silly' things just for the sake of it? Are you asking for too much? Is the bar set higher than it needs to be? Is the evaluation model itself too complicated?

It is always good to remember that the more complex a process, the more room for errors and challenge, and challenges on the issue of proportionality are not uncommon.

Azam & Co Solicitors v Legal Services Commission
This was a case that went to Appeal and I cite it here as an illustration of a claim of disproportionality mainly because I found it an odd one, but one which prompts thought on the subject.

Azam & Co (Azam) had their late tender submission for the provision of immigration services refused by the Legal Services Commission

(LSC). They took the case to court on the grounds that they had not been personally advised of the tender submission date. The High Court found against them and they went to the Court of Appeal – the work with LSC constituted the majority of their workload so the contract was very important to them.

Azam claimed that not advising them personally of the submission deadline lacked transparency and equality of treatment and that the refusal to accept their tender was disproportionate in that it had a far bigger impact on their commercial viability than the impact of accepting it would have had on the process. To me, I can see their point but it seems an odd logic to aver in a law case. What did the Court of Appeal think?

On the first couple of counts the court was clear – the dates for submission were posted clearly on the relevant websites and available to all. Azam should have made themselves aware of the due dates.

On the matter of proportionality, Azam claimed that extending the tender deadline was entirely within the LSC's control and their refusal to do this when asked to do so was disproportionate. The Judge opined that there was nothing disproportionate about LSC refusing to extend the deadline (i.e. 'change the tender rules') when the late submission was, in fact, wholly due to errors on the part of Azam. To have extended the deadline in such circumstances, he went on to say, would, in fact, have resulted in unequal treatment of the other bidders, who had noted the deadline and complied with it.

To me, this all seems logical, and the other Judges on the panel agreed wholeheartedly, but the Judge did make a couple of comments that I think are of interest. Firstly, he did acknowledge the serious financial impact the judgement would have on the plaintiff (Azam) and regretted this, but pointed out that despite his sympathies, there was no case in law. Secondly, he stated that there may well be instances when a refusal to accept a late submission might be deemed disproportionate in law (but this was not one). He cited *Leadbitter*, and we shall look at that one now.

J B Leadbitter & Co Ltd v Devon County Council

We last looked at the Leadbitter case with regards to late submissions (see Chapter 19). The case concerned documents accidentally omitted from Leadbitter's tender submission for a place on a construction framework: the council rejected the bid and Leadbitter challenged the decision.

Part of the grounds for the Leadbitter challenge was similar to those of Azam (above) in that they maintained that to reject a whole bid on the basis of a relatively small matter of a set of omitted documents was disproportionate to the 'misdemeanour' (my word) and so contravened that element of their duty[59] as a contracting authority.

Other cases had upheld challenges based on the issue of proportionality so the court noted that the issue of proportionality is one they may consider. That's precedents for you. However, the court decided that, in this case, refusal to accept the late submission was not acting disproportionately. It was interesting that the court opined that Devon could have accepted the late documents without disadvantaging the other bidders, but were in their right to decline them and so the claim was not allowed.

Let us look at one of the cases referred-to in the Leadbitter hearing.

Federal Security Services Ltd v The Northern Ireland Court Service

This case looks at proportionality in a totally different context and has some subtle undertones.

The Northern Ireland Court Service (NICS) issued a pre-qualification questionnaire as part of a negotiated tender process for the supply of security and other services to 23 courts in

---

59. Duty under the Recitals of Directive 2004/18

Northern Ireland. It issued a broad statement of requirements, to be firmed up in a Statement of Requirements later in the process. Federal Security Services Ltd (FSS) was one of 12 firms to submit a questionnaire and one of seven to be invited to tender.

At the end of this part of the process, FSS and another bidder, Maybin, were the preferred bidders, with Maybin ahead of FSS. Maybin was duly advised they had been successful and FSS were advised they had not, in the end, been appointed.

However, there was much debate in the civil service regarding whether the Maybin bid could be accepted because, at time of tender, the Statutory Security Licence they had submitted had expired, albeit a current licence was in place ready for the actual contract. The question was: was their bid valid at time of submission?

The Statement of Requirements stated that the tenderer must have a "Secretary of State Certificate/Licence" to provide the security services, a copy of which should be provided with the tender. This seems quite clear, except that, elsewhere in the documents, it stated that criteria, including mandatory requirements, would be scored and weighted. It is my personal view that a mandatory requirement cannot be scored – it has to be pass/fail – but that is what the documentation stated.

Proportionality? Don't worry – we're getting there.

The legal advice was that the requirements were not sufficiently clear, and that perfectly capable bidders could have taken the instructions to mean different things: the process was flawed on the grounds of transparency. It was also agreed that the award to Maybin was challengeable under the circumstances. On this basis, NICS decided to abandon the process and go for re-tender.

This is where FSS challenged on the grounds that abandoning the process was disproportionate to the issue. They maintained that the instructions were clear – a valid Certificate was required at time of tender – and so to scrap the whole process was over the top and, by the way, they were the second in line.

NICS argued that it was their duty to make sure that the process was transparent and that all bidders fully understood the process: this had not happened and so abandonment was the appropriate solution.

The court considered many arguments relating to the issue of transparency and mandatory requirements, but these points are not for us to debate here, save the court concurred on the need for clarity – of course – and felt that this had not been the case in this instance. On the matter of proportionality, they stated that the process was flawed to the extent that the outcome was completely unsafe – in other words, the procurement could not be saved and so abandonment was a valid decision, and one not taken lightly by the Contracting Authority.

NICS won, and abandoning the procurement was considered to be an act in proportion to the issue at hand – drastic, but proportionate.

The point of this chapter is to look at proportionality, but it raises many other issues as well, most of which boil down to getting the wording in the documents right. Regardless of the outcome, in our examples, delays and costs were incurred – as they always will be.

From these examples, it can be seen that issues of proportionality do crop up, albeit less frequently than other grounds for challenge, but it is a matter of which you should be aware. Keep the procurement as simple as you can and be careful not to overreact if a problem crops up - take considered and measured actions that are in proportion to the issue at hand.

What this means

> The concept of proportionality is sometimes hard for people to understand but it is what it says:

> Do not make demands or set standards that are out of proportion with what the procurement is aiming to achieve

> This can be apposite when qualification or evaluation criteria are being drawn up

> There is a link here to the chapter on eligibility (Chapter 13)

> A challenge of proportionality was raised when a tender went wrong and the authority decided to re-run the process – in other words, was this an overreaction on their part?

> In other words – do not crack walnuts with a sledgehammer and do not over complicate. It's simple, really. Remember the FLA – KISS[60]

Cases:

- *Azam & Co Solicitors v Legal services Commission [2010] EWCA Civ 1194*
- *J B Leadbitter & Co Ltd v Devon County Council ([2009] EWHC 930 (Ch)), judgment of 01 May 2009.*
- *Federal Security Services Ltd v The Northern Ireland Court Service ([2009] NIQB 15), judgment of 19 February 2009.*

---

60. FLA: a TLA meaning four letter acronym, which in this case means "Keep It Simple, Stupid", i.e. simple for them, simple for you, wherever possible.

CHAPTER 25 – SUICIDE BIDS

What are Suicide Bids?

Not being precisely what their name would imply, suicide bids are not made in the hopes of securing the demise of a company. Contrarily, they are bids designed to have the opposite effect and secure the immediate future of a firm struggling to survive. The trouble is, the bids are pitched excessively low to win the contract and enable the firm to benefit from the income, generating the cash flow it needs to continue.

Unfortunately, it rarely works (or it often doesn't – I do not have any actual statistics on the success of this tactic) either because firms are too far 'gone' for a couple of quick wins to save them or because, if you under-price work, you will not earn enough money to keep going. Hence the expression – a low bid can almost be another nail in the coffin.

In the cold light of just reading about it, this all seems logical but, when you have a company with employees and you are responsible for all of it, and it may all be turning to dust, the strategy of securing cash flow through low bids in an effort to save it all is understandable. It does happen a lot, and more so in times of recession, of course.

Having said that, just because a bid is low it does not always mean the bidder is on the verge of bankruptcy. Sometimes there are other, more legitimate reasons such as securing an 'in' with a particular client or getting a foothold in a particular part of the country. Sometimes, of course, it is simply a mistake.

So what to do? In general terms, if you find a bid is seemingly too low (and especially if it is likely to win on that basis) you need to approach the bidder to confirm the price. You may even require them to produce proof (e.g. a business case) showing how they can submit such a low bid and make it work. If they can demonstrate it, you are virtually obliged to accept the bid, even if it is against your better judgement or gut feeling to do so. To refuse such a bid when the bidder has made the case could lead to a challenge that would be hard to defend.

It can be a difficult situation. Let us look at some examples.

Morrison Facilities Services Limited v Norwich City Council
The tender was for a contract to provide a repairs service to social housing for Norwich City Council (Norwich). Morrison Facilities Services Limited (Morrison) was the incumbent and submitted a bid but lost to Connaught Partnerships Ltd (Connaught).

Morrison raised a challenge at the outcome of the tender on the grounds that Norwich used undisclosed criteria as part of the evaluation process and that Connaught's winning bid was too low to be viable. We are only going to look at the second matter here.

The facts of the costings are that submitted bids ranged in value between £23million and £26million apart from Connaught, who came in at £17.5 million - £5.5million lower than the next bid. Further, Morrison advised that Norwich had twice, during the course of the evaluation, asked Connaught to confirm its tender sum. However, despite this, Norwich had failed to properly investigate the bid as being sustainable, as they ought to have done[61].

The Court agreed there was a case to be tried:

- The Council did have doubts about the Connaught bid
- It is arguable in law that the Contracting Authority does have a duty to investigate an abnormally low tender
- There appeared to be no explanation of how the Connaught figures made a viable bid
- The Council had so far submitted no evidence to prove that it had taken steps to verify the viability of the Connaught bid.

An interesting addition to this case is that Morrison argued that

---

61. Regulation 30(6) of the 2006 Regulations and Article 55 of Directive 2004/18

damages would not be an adequate remedy, stressing that actual losses by the parties would be hard to identify and referring to the case of Letting International *v* LB Newham (see earlier Chapter 9). It seems to me they were looking for the Connaught bid to be discounted or the tender re-run (second-best option – costs of the tender exercise may be claimable).

There were various arguments around this point but we do not need to consider them here. Oh yes – the outcome? Morrison settled its dispute with Norwich and so the case did not proceed to court (so no actual judgement) and Connaught went into administration in September of that year[62].

Despite the lack of judgement, the points raised by the case are still as valid. We will briefly look at them.

Morrison cited regulatory requirements to investigate low bids – or seemed to. In fact, Regulation 30 (6) of the Regulations gives the Contracting Authority the right to reject an abnormally low tender subject to giving the bidder a chance to justify it. Rejection is not an outright right or requirement, if you know what I mean.

From another angle, the EU Treaty requires all bidders to be treated equally. To allow a bid to succeed because the tenderer has not priced it properly (deliberately or otherwise) is not fair on those who have done it correctly, and so the requirement for equal treatment is breached. That is an aspect of equal treatment of bidders that is not often cited.

The matter gives rise to the question of how do you determine an 'abnormally low bid'? There are no rules, but in the case of Morrison, Connaught's bid was 25% lower than the next bid, when all the others were closely clustered – that *has* to warrant examination. That is the most common yardstick – what does the market tell you a bid *ought* to be?

62. You may recall that Connaught's demise caused major problems in the Social Housing Sector as they had won a vast portfolio of contracts – seemingly with many of them secured through low bids.

Otherwise, you can do some intelligent pre-tender estimating (PTE) and use that as a guide, but if *all* the bids come in 'abnormally low' do you investigate them all or do you reckon your PTE was high in the first place? My bet is on the latter.

One further rider to this – if you are using MEAT criteria and a very low bid is supported by very low quality marks, then that may give you the answer as to how such a low price was achieved. If the evaluation model is good and the documentation worded appropriately, they will not be in line for award anyway, so no problem.

On the matter of sustainable bid prices, I refer you to the Virgin Challenge of DfT over the award of the West Coast Rail Route, in Chapter 4 on Challenges. Whilst Chapter 4 deals with the process of Challenge and timeliness of actions, the case itself is based on the financial sustainability of a winning tender: it was not suicide bidding but the bid was argued as low and the reasoning and the challenge are both relevant and interesting.

What this means

> In fact, suicide bids are rare but they do crop up. However, surprisingly low bids do crop up quite regularly

> Where a bid appears unviable, you are obliged to seek proof that the bid is genuine and the bidder can deliver successfully at that price – and the bidder has to respond. If they do not or cannot, you can reject the bid

> Where you have only two tender returns and one is much lower than the other, claiming one is ridiculously low or the other is outrageously high is difficult: even pre-tender estimates can be way off the mark so do not necessarily serve as a guide. For this reason, a minimum of three submissions should be assessed wherever possible

> When awarding to a very low bid, the management of that contract may need to step up a gear at least until the provider has proven themselves – and they often do

> Sometimes unsuccessful bidders may challenge on the basis that the winner's submission is unviable so the need for good diligence on your part is paramount as you may well have to defend the decision to award

---

Cases:

- *Morrison Facilities Services Limited v Norwich City Council [2010] EWHC 487 (CH), judgment of Arnold J 22 February 2010*

CHAPTER 26 – TERMINATION

Isn't termination simply a matter of imposing a clause in a contract?
This is a brief chapter on the subject of terminating a contract on the grounds of a breach, included because: no - it is not always as simple as it may at first appear.

Termination clauses are very important and are seen as an effective contract management tool in maintaining provider performance and a contingency in the event that the contract – or rather the contractor – goes 'bad'. It is the 'get-out' clause that mitigates the risk of being captured in a contractual marriage made in hell.

Unfortunately, care needs to be taken: the law is a little odd on this matter and often the litigant attempting to terminate the contract (i.e. maybe you) becomes the defendant as the tables are turned upon them.

As a cautionary tale, we will look at the case of *Lonsdale*. It was a long, drawn out affair, so I shall summarise it so that only the salient points come to the fore.

Leofelis SA and another v Lonsdale Sports Ltd and others and *Trademark Licensing Company Ltd and another v Leofelis SA and others*
The case centred on the granting of an exclusive license by Lonsdale Sports Ltd (Lonsdale) to Leofelis to use their trademark in certain countries of Europe. This was in 2002. By 2005, Leofelis had started litigation on the basis that Lonsdale had committed a repudiatory breach of the contract. A repudiatory breach is a breach of a clause that is fundamental to the contract and one such that claims for damages, such as loss of profit, may be lodged.

The case rattled around in various forms until 2012, when the latest (not final at time of going to print, note) judgement was made. This judgement and its history is what deserves our consideration.

Originally, Lonsdale had managed to demonstrate that the Leofelis claim was unfounded and the judge found in favour of Lonsdale. Leofelis came back and said – in so many words – OK, they may have been in the right on that point, but what about *this* point? During the course of the hearing, Lonsdale had demonstrated that they had also granted a trademark license to another firm operating in Latvia – this was a repudiatory breach and in this instance the court found in favour of Leofelis.

The court accepted that the (new) ground for termination justified the original notice of termination but – and this is the big but – because the ground was discovered after the original notice and not cited as part of it, they ruled that damages for loss of profit, etc., which were part of the suit, could not be awarded. For the logic, I shall quote the judge[63] who said: *"the alleged breach, although its nature met the test for a repudiatory breach, cannot be the cause of the termination and therefore of the loss that flowed from the termination."*

Translating this, whilst the claim of breach was upheld and so the Notice of Termination (NOT) upheld, the breach was not the breach cited in the NOT so could not be the basis of the attendant claims for losses emanating from the NOT.

Thus, Leofelis were successful in terminating the contract but got no money out of it – not even costs – and so commercially the suit was not, as it turned out, 'a good move', so to speak.

Thus, when seeking to terminate, you can call on any breaches you unearth even after the NOT is issued, but don't rely on recouping any costs or losses.

This account and the conclusion (to date) with respect to Notices of Termination in general depends on two things: firstly, that the contract termination ends up going to court (it does not have to)

---

63. Roth J

and secondly that the summary judgement[64] handed down (above) will not be overturned or superseded by a later judgement: it is generally thought that this might be the case (no pun intended). We can only wait and see.

What this means

> Do try and avoid legal action on the grounds of a breach – where possible try and address the matter and manage the contract out of the situation

> Sometimes the breach can be due to poor contract management on the client's part and the legal tables can be turned

> Breaches are best avoided by ensuring that the tender process and the contract are both clear on the contract's requirements and cater for all the needs that the contract was intended to deliver

> Include remedies for failure other than plain termination – always leave wriggle-room, although a termination clause should always be included as the ultimate management tool available to the client

> Termination clauses are different to get-out clauses, which serve a different purpose and should be drawn up such that they minimise the adverse impact on all parties to the contract

> Beware instigating termination in a fit of pique – it is not something that, once started, can be easily rescinded and may be an action that works out worse for the client than the ex-provider.

---

64. A Judge's opinion, based on facts in law, sought or given in an attempt to avoid the costs and time of a full trial with evidence and witnesses.

Case:

- *Leofelis SA and another v Lonsdale Sports and others; Trademark Licensing Company Ltd and another v Leofelis and others [2012] EWHC 485 (Ch), 9 March 2012*

CONCLUSION – OF CASES

Chapter 26 marks the end of our look at court cases and the precedents set as a result of them. We shall now move on to a consideration of some of the more recent pieces of legislation as a heads-up on what to beware of especially where, in many instances, case law has not yet fully tested the law and established best practice.

LEGISLATION

The following six chapters give a brief overview of some pieces of legislation that are key to procurement. The list – again – is my own eclectic choice and the information given is not legal guidance but is designed to give the reader an idea of what the legislation covers and its key requirements for the procurement practitioner.

For more detailed coverage of these acts and directives, the reader is recommended to refer to the cabinet office website at:

http://www.cabinetoffice.gov.uk/

where Procurement Policy Notes will provide more in-depth guidance, or search the actual acts themselves via the internet using a search engine or the links provided.

Another useful website – of which you are probably already aware – is Europa, in particular Simap, which is a mine of useful information. Simap can be found at:

http://simap.europa.eu/index_en.htm

CHAPTER 27 – THE BRIBERY ACT

The updated Bribery Act came into force on the 1st July 2011. It puts greater onus onto the contracting authority to guard against and prevent bribery and corruption.

Whilst contracts for most normal people like us are not as liable to bribery as some aerospace contracts in the Emirates might be, there is still a legal obligation to actively take preventive measures.

In principle, an organisation has a responsibility use 'adequate measures' to prevent bribery and corruption by any 'associated person' – and they could become associated simply through participating in a procurement process you are running.

Failure to prevent a bribe or demonstrate that it occurred despite your 'adequate measures' can lead to unlimited fines being imposed on any organisation involved, mean prison for individuals found complicit, bar the bidder from tendering for public contracts in the future (no time limit set) and still have the contract in question set aside (i.e. cancelled).

So what are 'adequate measures' in the eyes of the law? In principle they comprise a risk assessment then procedures proportionate to the risk; top-level commitment should be supported by due diligence and communication, monitoring and reviews. It is also recommended that training is undertaken.

It also means that non-collusion and non-corruption clauses in PQQ and tender documentation need to be reviewed and tightened up if considered appropriate and individuals should be more cautious about offers of hospitality from firms who tender with us.

Note, however, that the Government recently issued some guidance that 'eased up' on the acceptance of minor 'gifts' as goodwill gestures so, as usual, we have to rely on the court cases that arise to guide us on how wary we have to be.

In the meantime – be prudent.

Further guidance can be found via a Ministry of Justice publication at:

https://www.gov.uk/government/uploads/system/uploads/ attachment_data/file/181762/bribery-act-2010-guidance.pdf

---

CHAPTER 28 – COMPETITION ACT

The Competition Act 2010 (latest amended version) is generally upheld through the Office of Fair Trading (OFT); any breaches of EU Law in respect of uncompetitive behaviour are generally dealt with using the law of the land where the breach took place and because of this OFT has strong links with the ECJ.

The Act has quite a hefty clout and firms found in breach of its requirements can be fined up to 10% of their global turnover: that's hefty.

Damages from effected third parties can also ensue and eligibility to tender under Regulation 23 may also be impacted, depending on the nature of the infringement.

The Act has two principle thrusts. One relates to disproportionate market dominance, which is not relevant to our concerns here, but the other concerns anti-competitive agreements (collusion) which is very relevant. If such behaviour involves other member states, the perpetrator is in breach of Articles 101 and 102 of the Treaty on the Functioning of the European Union (TFEU).

To 'cover' yourself in any procurement, all returns – either at pre-selection or tender stage – should be submitted under cover of a declaration of probity and non-collusion. This, in the form of a 'Form of Tender' should be well-known to you, but you must ensure a similar declaration is made at PQQ stage as well. Not to do so could be perceived as a lack in due diligence.

More information can be found at:

http://www.oft.gov.uk/

CHAPTER 29 – REGULATION 23

Regulation 23 of the Public Contracts Regulations 2006 forbids a person or a company who has a history of fraud, collusion or financial misdemeanours from bidding for a public contract. More importantly, it also precludes us – other than in very extenuating circumstances – from inviting to tender any organisation or individual who fails against the stringent criteria that the Act lays down.

To safeguard yourself and your organisation, it is wise to issue a declaration to the effect that anyone who contravenes the requirements of Regulation 23 should not bid, and seeking confirmation from all potential bidders, within the PQQ, that they comply (a simple yes/no tick box will suffice – it is still a declaration, signed off at the end).

Rejection of a bidder or an Applicant is expected (my expression) when the contractor, its directors or any other person who has powers of representation, decision or control of the contractor has been convicted of any one of a range of offences. The Regulation itself says:

Criteria for the rejection of economic operators

23. (1) Subject to paragraph (2), a contracting authority shall treat as ineligible and shall not select an economic operator in accordance with these Regulations if the contracting authority has actual knowledge that the economic operator or its directors or any other person who has powers of representation, decision or control of the economic operator has been convicted of any of the following offences:

(a) conspiracy within the meaning of section 1 or 1A of the Criminal Law Act 1977 where that conspiracy relates to participation in a criminal organisation as defined in Article 2 of Council Framework Decision 2008/841/ JHA;

(b)　corruption within the meaning of section 1(2) of the Public Bodies Corrupt Practices Act 1889 or section 1 of the Prevention of Corruption Act 1906, where the offence relates to active corruption;

(c)　the offence of bribery, where the offence relates to active corruption[65];

(d)　fraud, where the offence relates to fraud affecting the financial interests of the European Communities as defined by Article 1 of the Convention on the protection of the financial interests of the European Communities, within the meaning of:

i)　the offence of cheating the Revenue;

ii)　the offence of conspiracy to defraud;

iii)　fraud or theft within the meaning of the Theft Act 1968 and the Theft Act 1978

iv)　fraudulent trading within the meaning of section 458 of the Companies Act 1985[66]

v) defrauding the Customs within the meaning of the Customs and Excise Management Act 1979 and the Value Added Tax Act 1994;

vi) an offence in connection with taxation in the European Union within the meaning of section 71 of the Criminal Justice Act 1993; or

vii) destroying, defacing or concealing of documents or procuring the execution of a valuable security within the meaning of section 20 of the Theft Act 1968

(e)　money laundering within the meaning of the Money Laundering Regulations 2003;

any other offence within the meaning of Article 45(1) of the Public Sector Directive as defined by the national law of any relevant State

---

65. Bribery within the meaning of section 1 or 6 of the Bribery Act 2010
66. Or section 993 of the Companies Act 2006

(2) In any case where an economic operator or its directors or any other person who has powers of representation, decision or control has been convicted of an offence described in paragraph (1), a contracting authority may disregard the prohibition described there if it is satisfied that there are overriding requirements in the general interest which justify doing so in relation to that economic operator.

(3) A contracting authority may apply to the relevant competent authority to obtain further information regarding the economic operator and in particular details of convictions of the offences listed in paragraph (1) if it considers it needs such information to decide on any exclusion referred to in that paragraph.

(4) A contracting authority may treat an economic operator as ineligible or decide not to select an economic operator in accordance with these Regulations on one or more of the following grounds, namely that the economic operator –

    (a)   being an individual is a person in respect of whom a debt relief order has been made or is bankrupt or has had a receiving order or administration order or bankruptcy restrictions order or a debt relief order made against him or has made any composition or arrangement with or for the benefit of his creditors or has made any conveyance or assignment for the benefit of his creditors or appears unable to pay, or to have no reasonable prospect of being able to pay, a debt within the meaning of section 268 of the Insolvency Act 1986 (as amended) or article 242 of the Insolvency (Northern Ireland) Order 1989 (as amended), or in Scotland has granted a trust deed for creditors or become otherwise apparently insolvent, or is the subject of a petition presented for sequestration of his estate, or is the subject of any similar procedure under the law of any other state;

(b)   being a partnership constituted under Scots law has granted a trust deed or become otherwise apparently insolvent, or is the subject of a petition presented for sequestration of its estate;

(c)   being a company or any other entity within the meaning of section 255 of the Enterprise Act 2002 (as amended) has passed a resolution or is the subject of an order by the court for the company's winding up otherwise than for the purpose of bona fide reconstruction or amalgamation, or has had a receiver, manager or administrator on behalf of a creditor appointed in respect of the company's business or any part thereof or is the subject of the above procedures or is the subject of similar procedures under the law of any other state;

(d)   has been convicted of a criminal offence relating to the conduct of his business or profession

(e)   has committed an act of grave misconduct in the course of his business or profession;

(f)   has not fulfilled obligations relating to the payment of social security contributions under the law of any part of the United Kingdom or of the relevant state in which the contractor is established;

(g)   has not fulfilled obligations relating to the payment of taxes under the law of any part of the United Kingdom or of the relevant state in which the contractor is established;

(h)   is guilty of serious misrepresentation in providing any information required of him under this regulation;

(i)   in relation to the procedures for the award of a public services contract, is not licensed in the relevant state in which he is established or is not a member of an organisation in that relevant state when the law of that relevant state prohibits the provision of the services to be provided under the contract by a person who is not licensed or who is not such a member; or

(j)   is not registered on the professional or trade register of the relevant state in which he is established under conditions laid down by that state.

Paragraphs 5 to 9 follow but are not so directly relevant here except that Paragraphs 5 and 6, along with Paragraphs 2 and 3 above, lay down that

a.   a contracting authority is entitled to seek information on a bidder's history in the context of implementing the requirements of this Regulation, and also...
b.   the contracting authority has leeway to accept the firm in question as a bidder if they can provide sufficient evidence to demonstrate that the individual/s concerned is/are indispensable (my phrase) to the procurement or the contract. Accepting any such argument is discretionary.

This last piece, to my mind, can be a bit of a red herring – I would not like to have to make the final say regarding a firm's eligibility to bid in these circumstances because, in my mind, I am neither equipped nor qualified to determine the importance of a particular individual's rôle in a procurement nor especially their proclivity towards criminal dealings in the future.

I will not elaborate on these points any further but suggest you follow the link at the bottom of this chapter for the whole story.

I have reproduced most of Regulation 23 here verbatim in order to stress its emphatic nature. I suggest, however, that if you are going to include guidance on this in your documents, you would be well advised to paraphrase it somewhat and specifically refer bidders to the Act itself so that they may confirm for themselves whether or not they are eligible to tender before self-certifying as part of their submission. I would be wary of accepting any pleas for an exemption from the Regulation's requirements.

More details on Regulation 23 can be found at:

http://www.legislation.gov.uk/uksi/2006/5/regulation/23/made

CHAPTER 30 – REMEDIES DIRECTIVE

Mentioned more than once in this book, The Remedies Directive[67] gave the procurement world a big scare when it first came out because, given the right circumstances, challenges based on it could lead to an executed contract being cancelled, full stop.

In reality, the majority of the Amendments are relatively minor and tend to more-clearly define existing requirements, but some of the new provisions are quite stringent.

These additional regulations are laid down in Regulation 47, Paragraphs A to M, and essentially define additional powers of UK courts to take action in the event of a breach in a procurement process.

We shall first take a summary view of the legislation and then go into it in more detail.

<u>In Summary</u>

The Directive provides for measures under two specific circumstances:

1. After award of contract and
2. Before award of contract

1. *After you have entered into a contract* the courts will have the power to:

   - Issue a Declaration of Ineffectiveness (i.e. declare the contract void)
   - Impose Civil Financial Penalties
   - Award damages

---

67. Officially: The Public Contracts (Amendment) Regulations 2009 – becoming law on 20th December of that year.

It should be noted that a Declaration of Ineffectiveness is *mandatory* if any of the specific 'grounds of ineffectiveness' are proven. These grounds are:

- Failure to publish a Contract Notice (OJEU advert) when required
- Contract entered into in breach of Standstill (Alcatel) requirements
- Contract entered into in breach of a Court Order or proceedings
- Contract awarded under a Framework in breach of Regulations governing competition and price thresholds.

The only mitigations for not imposing mandatory ineffectiveness are where:

- The ineffectiveness would be contrary to 'general interest' or the common good and / or
- Such action would have a disproportionate adverse impact.

Disproportionate adverse impacts on the contract itself would *not* be considered suitable mitigation.

In practice, a contract will not be set aside immediately, but after an appropriate period of time to enable a new provision to be put in place. Such consideration will take into account the 'common good'.

1. *Before you have entered into a contract* a Court will have the powers to:

- Set aside any decision or action (e.g. decision to award)
- Order the amendment of any document
- Award damages to any Economic Operator suffering loss or damage.

Such actions will be without prejudice to any other powers of Court – so consequential or additional claims may still arise.

A more detailed consideration of all these points follows.

<u>The Directive in More Detail</u>

All the points given in the summary above have various caveats and consequences attached and these are covered in this section under the specific headings.

Grounds for Ineffectiveness
There are caveats qualifying the validity of the Grounds for Ineffectiveness listed above.

Ground: Failure to publish a Contract Notice (OJEU advert) when required is *not* a ground when an Authority:

a. Considers a Notice was not required *and*
b. Publishes a Voluntary Transparency Notice (VTN) *and*
c. Does not enter into a contract for 10 days following the VTN.

Ground: Contract entered in to in breach of Standstill (Alcatel) requirements *only* applies if:

a. Breach has deprived an operator of pre-contractual remedies *and*
b. There has been a substantial separate breach of the Regulations *and*
c. This has affected the operator's chances of winning.

Ground: A contract entered into in breach of a Court Order or proceedings by definition means that the process was legally void and so there are no mitigations.

Ground: When awarded under a Framework in breach of Regulations governing competition and price thresholds (Regs 8, 19 and 20[68]), grounds for ineffectiveness will apply *unless*:
a. The Authority considers itself to be compliant *and*

---

68. Public Contract Regulations 2006 – The 'EU Regs'.

b.   Undertakes a voluntary standstill period *and*
c.   Does not enter into a contract until the expiry of this standstill period.

Timescales

The Directive lays down timescales within which an Action must be taken.

When the action is <u>*not*</u> seeking a declaration of ineffectiveness, an Action must be started:

- Promptly and, anyway:
- within 3 months of the date when the grounds for action occurred

However, the Regulations do not require proceedings to be started before:

- Ten days after the date on which the company was notified of the decision *and*
- After it has been given the reasons for that decision.

This means either not before the end of the Alcatel or Standstill period (covered in Regulation 32)[69] *or* 10 days after the date *on which that Economic Operator* in particular was informed of the tender outcome in the manner above.

When the Action <u>*is*</u> seeking a declaration of ineffectiveness, an Action must be started:

- Within 30 days of an operator being advised of the conclusion of a contract and being given the relevant reasons *or*,
- Where the contract is already in effect, within 6 months of the day after the contract was entered into *or*
- Within 30 days of the publication of a Contract Award Notice

---

69. These timescales (above) are for decisions transmitted electronically. If the decision is *not* issued electronically, other timescales apply. Refer to the Regulations.

This last one applies if – and only if –

a. The contract was awarded without a Contract Notice (i.e. OJEU advert) *and*
b. The Contract Award Notice includes justification for there being no OJEU advert.

Powers of the Courts
The type of Action a court can take will (obviously) depend upon the stage the tender or contract has reached.

Where a contract *has not* been entered into, depending on the nature of the breach, courts can:

- Set aside a decision or an action
- Order documents to be amended
- Award damages to an Economic Operator (company) suffering loss or damage.

Such actions are without prejudice to other powers of court, i.e. such actions do not prevent other legal actions being taken.

If the contract *has* been awarded the Courts *have* to declare the contract ineffective where grounds are proven. Only where the mitigations explained above apply can a Declaration of Ineffectiveness be avoided.

When a Declaration of Ineffectiveness is imposed, a civil penalty might also be levied.

A penalty or a shortening of the contract must be imposed when

a. a Declaration of Ineffectiveness applies but mitigations prevent its imposition or
b. a contract was awarded during a standstill period or
c. a contract was awarded in breach of a Court Order or Suspension

Penalties (paid to HM Treasury) or shortenings must be effective (i.e. dissuasive) and proportionate, having regard to the seriousness of the breach, the behaviour of the Authority and the extent to which the contract remains in force.

These considerations apply to the totality of all penalties imposed as a result of more than one complaint.

Damages
Damages are awarded where an Economic operator has suffered loss or damage and can be *in addition* to any other measures imposed.

For further information, the full set of Amendments can be downloaded at:

http://www.opsi.gov.uk/si/si2009/uksi_20092992_en_1

CHAPTER 31 – SOCIAL VALUE ACT

The Public Services (Social Value) Act 2012 requires economic, environmental and social benefits of a procurement to be considered as part of the strategic approach to the process of a services contract tender.

It is considered that encompassing these aspects into the tender will help ensure that maximum value for money has been achieved and appropriate consultation should be entered into.

The Act has two key aspects:

1. The Act only applies to services (Part A and Part B) as defined in the Public Contracts Regulations 2006 (the EU Regs)
2. The Act only applies to procurement processes for services covered by the EU Regulations, i.e. those over the EU threshold
3. The Act requires the procuring authority to *consider* what social benefits may be gleaned from the tender

Only social values relevant to the service need be considered and only to the extent that it is proportionate to the service and its contract. There is no compulsion to 'find something to include' and the Act is unprescriptive in how a procurement should accommodate any social improvement aspects.

There is no specific requirement to report back on social improvement measures incorporated into any procurement, but a log of any such improvements may be of benefit if your procurement team is brought to task on the matter.

My personal view is that such 'extras' do tend to cost money and the contracting authority – in particular those with the purse strings, as stakeholders to the procurement strategy for the service concerned – needs to be made aware of this.

The Local Government Act, 1999, defines Best Value as: *"...to secure continuous improvement in the way in which its functions are exercised, having regard to a combination of economy, efficiency and effectiveness."* Under this requirement, overall value comprises environmental and social value.

Further Guidance on The Social Value Act can be found at:

https://www.gov.uk/government/publications/procurement-policy-note-10-12-the-public-services-social-value-act-2012

and more information on Best Value can be found in the Communities and Local Government's publication "Best Value Duty"

CHAPTER 32 – NEW DIRECTIVE 2014

A new procurement directive is has been agreed in Europe and is currently (at time of print) being incorporated into the laws of the lands of the European Union. Adoption by UK law is expected in October 2014 and note I say 'expected'.

There has been much speculation regarding what the Directive will contain: some of it is fairly certain but a lot of it all remains speculation nevertheless until the final adopted form is known.

The Cabinet Office is a good source of information on the current situation but I shall refrain from giving any information on what the Directive is going to say because we just don't know – it would be a waste of time.

I'll just say this: be aware that it is coming and when it appears learn fast because its requirements will apply to any procurement that is commenced after its adoption in law. This is a particularly poignant point because it seems that a lot of the changes will be beneficial to the procurement process (that is the whole point of the Directive) and early adoption of the new Regulations and realisation of its benefits should perhaps be paramount.

There will doubtless be some disagreement over what some of it actually means – there always is – and so, once again, we shall have to wait and see how the courts interpret the Directive's meanings and intentions.

That is how it all works.

CONCLUSION – FINAL

Keeping up

The purpose of this book was to show you how procurement practice, and its compliance with the law, is directly influenced by the decisions taken in the courts. Accordingly, you should consider it part of your day job to keep abreast of these decisions.

One way you can do this is by signing up for case briefings and legal updates from law firms who specialise in procurement, and they are usually more than happy to send them to you on a regular basis. There are several firms you can contact but I have to refrain from naming any here – you will need to carry out your own research on this.

Also, as advised earlier, you can check the Cabinet Office's website for their Procurement Policy Notes (PPNs), which provide regular updates on EU Procurement Law. The direct link to PPNs is:

https://www.gov.uk/government/collections/procurement-policy-notes

I suggest you bookmark the page and visit it regularly.

PPNs can be downloaded and saved and they can be distributed to team members, although you may need to sort the wheat from the chaff to ensure that what you give out is recognised as relevant, otherwise people will tend to ignore them.

I hope all the foregoing will be of use to you in your everyday procurement life but remember that the law tweaks and changes things on an almost daily basis: the outcome of a new case can bring a different slant on something that has been accepted as standard practice for years, and a whole new approach may suddenly be required.

That is what this book is about – and that's the fun of procurement[70].

70. Wry humour.

Alphabetical List of Cases

Index

Printed in Great Britain
by Amazon.co.uk, Ltd.,
Marston Gate.